THE
ASTROLOGICAL
SELF-CARE
JOURNAL

FIND COSMIC GUIDANCE & INSIGHT
TO TAKE CARE OF YOU

STEPHANIE GAILING

ROCK
POINT

contents

introduction

YEARS AGO, TO MY DELIGHT, I discovered that there was a healing art that combined two of my greatest passions: astrology and health. Always looking for ways to inspire people to achieve their optimal well-being, I embarked on learning more about this system of healing.

With a long and illustrious past, this approach to optimizing well-being—known as medical astrology—views planetary placements as a guide for assessing health and proposing therapeutic treatments. It was documented by ancient Greek scholars, taught in medieval medical schools, practiced by Renaissance physicians, and, until the early twentieth century, used by many doctors alongside other health-care methods. The study of the stars was so integral to the work of many healers that Hippocrates, considered the father of modern medicine, was noted to have said, "He who does not understand astrology is not a doctor but a fool."

Yet, I've come to realize that astrology's application to health doesn't need to be limited to diagnosing and treating illness. I've seen how its fundamental tenets can be applied to the realm of self-care, used as a framework to help us tap into more energy, reduce stress, and feel more aligned.

At the heart of wellness astrology is the axiom "as above, so below," reflecting the long-held belief in the connection between the celestial bodies and our own bodies. Throughout history, the zodiac signs and their ruling planets have been associated with various body parts, emotional tendencies, and personality temperaments, and even have signature correspondences with different members of the plant kingdom.

In addition to astrology helping us to decode our personal self-care needs based upon our star chart, knowing which planets and signs are playing a key role in the sky at any time can help us zero in on the invitations that different moments offer; this itself allows us to orient in ways that minimize stress and optimize well-being throughout the year.

The Astrological Self-care Journal embodies this astrological approach to wellness. As different moments in time—reflected by New Moons, Full Moons, and Planetary Retrogrades and Stations—provide us with unique opportunities for learning and understanding, this journal will help you sequence your self-care in a stellar way. It will guide you through the year, aligning you with the times so you can be more aware of the opportunities present at distinct moments while also giving you strategies to sidestep stress. Additionally, it is a resource to help you tune into yourself—and what you need to feel your very best—by sharing insights about your zodiac signs.

To me, self-care is not only about the activities we do, foods we eat, and remedies we use, but also about taking steps to orient to life with enhanced consciousness and awareness. I believe that one of the most treasured ways to access this knowledge is through inquiry practices and journaling questions, such as the Stellar Reflections included throughout this book. They will guide you to access the rich wisdom that resides within you, assisting you in optimizing your well-being.

how to use this journal

THIS JOURNAL PROVIDES you with self-care insights and writing prompts, called Stellar Reflections, that align with celestial events that occur during the year, as well as each zodiac sign. You'll find this journal to be a resource you turn to again and again to help you navigate a multiplicity of moments that you'll experience over time.

You can discover the dates for the celestial events featured in the first three sections—The Moons, Planetary Retrogrades, and Planetary Stations—in the Celestial Event Calendar section on page 158. For the Zodiac Signs section, you can cast your astrology chart—and find your Sun, Moon, and Ascendant signs—at astro.com or sodivine.us.

The Moons

The Moons section includes insights into the 24 unique New and Full Moons that occur annually; as each is defined by the zodiac sign that the Sun and Moon are in, each offers us unique opportunities for learning as well as special self-care considerations.

A few days before each monthly New Moon and Full Moon, read the corresponding pages so you can start to tap in to the energies that are being ushered in. Then on the day of, or just after, each lunation, read through the affirmations and self-care rituals, and get inspired by the Stellar Reflections journaling prompts.

Planetary Retrogrades

In this section, you'll find insights to help you make the most of Mercury, Venus, and Mars Retrograde. As each of these planetary cycles lasts several weeks, you can work through the pages at any time and/or come back to them numerous times during the planet's retrograde period. While in a given year we may have one Venus or Mars Retrograde, there are three annual Mercury Retrograde periods. Each time it occurs during the year, you can use these pages as a wayfinding tool.

Planetary Stations

Of all the realms included in this journal, Planetary Stations may be the one you're least familiar with—and yet, being aware of these celestial happenings can do wonders for enhancing your well-being. Each of the included stations—for Jupiter, Saturn, Uranus, Neptune, and Pluto—usually occurs twice each year; as such, you can work with these pages at these biannual junctures.

Zodiac Signs

To gain personalized stellar insights that can help you foster your well-being, turn to the pages that address your Sun sign, and the signs of your Moon and Ascendant if you know those as well. All three will help you gain stellar self-care awareness, since your Sun sign represents what lights you up, your Moon sign reflects how you orient emotionally, and your Ascendant sign symbolizes the way that you present yourself to the world, and therefore some of your physical characteristics.

THE MOONS

Being in concert with the rhythms of the lunar cycle can help us
feel more aligned. Whether it's honoring beginnings at the New
Moon or perceiving fruition at the Full Moon, there's a feeling of
ease that arises when we're in tune with the Moon as it moves through
the different signs of the zodiac. On the following pages, you'll learn
about the opportunities and challenges that each of the different
New and Full Moons hold. To help you tap into their invitation
for healing, you'll find journaling prompts that are in alignment
with each. These will help you invite in awareness while also
side-stepping stress, using the Moon as a guiding light that can
chaperone you on your journey to optimal well-being.

Aries New Moon

THE OPPORTUNITIES INCLUDE:

- Finding the courage to begin something you've been avoiding.
- Discovering a cause for which you want to fight.

THE CHALLENGES INCLUDE:

- Moving fast could lead to minor accidents or mishaps.
- A now-or-never orientation may catalyze a rash of impatience, irritation, and anger.

AFFIRMATIONS

- I lay claim to my desires.
- I am brave.
- I am energized.
- The present moment informs me deeply.

SELF-CARE RITUALS

- Exercise outdoors.
- Add some spice to your meals.

Celestial Event Calendar Page 158

STELLAR REFLECTIONS

What do I want to champion?

....
....
....
....
....
....
....
....

What can help me be more patient?

....
....
....
....
....
....
....
....

STELLAR REFLECTIONS

What incites my passion?

....
....
....
....
....
....
....
....

How can I better assert myself when necessary?

....
....
....
....
....
....
....
....
....

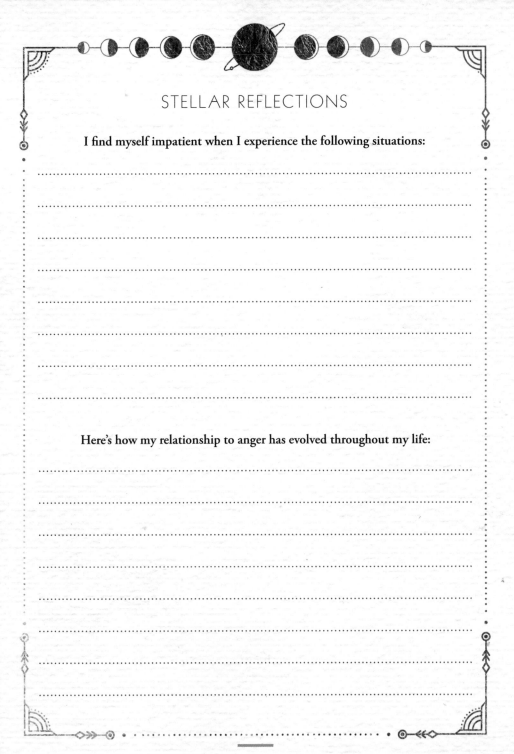

STELLAR REFLECTIONS

I find myself impatient when I experience the following situations:

....

....

....

....

....

....

....

....

Here's how my relationship to anger has evolved throughout my life:

....

....

....

....

....

....

....

....

Taurus New Moon

THE OPPORTUNITIES INCLUDE:

- Surveying your habits to see which are truly supportive.
- Looking to nature for guidance and grounding.

THE CHALLENGES INCLUDE:

- A swell of stubbornness limits adaptability.
- A focus on the mundane overrides the ability to look under the surface.

AFFIRMATIONS

- My senses delight and inform me.
- Being practical yields great possibilities.
- The Earth supports and nurtures me.
- I am safe.

SELF-CARE RITUALS

- Listen to music.
- Buy yourself flowers.

Celestial Event Calendar Page 158

STELLAR REFLECTIONS

What does security mean to me?

....

....

....

....

....

....

....

....

What do I consider to be the epitome of a pleasurable experience?

....

....

....

....

....

....

....

....

STELLAR REFLECTIONS

How can I forge a deeper connection to the Earth?

....

....

....

....

....

....

....

What new health habit would I like to adopt, and why?

....

....

....

....

....

....

....

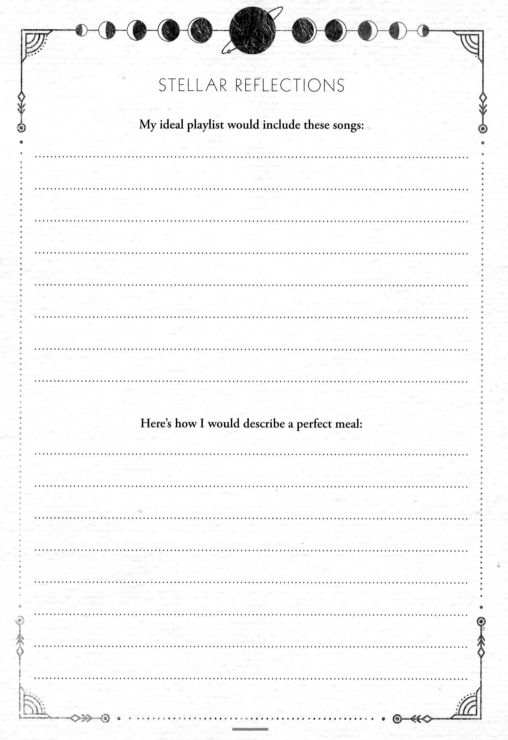

STELLAR REFLECTIONS

My ideal playlist would include these songs:

....

....

....

....

....

....

....

....

....

Here's how I would describe a perfect meal:

....

....

....

....

....

....

....

....

....

Gemini New Moon

THE OPPORTUNITIES INCLUDE:

- Discovering solutions through conversations.
- Flexibility and versatility become assets.

THE CHALLENGES INCLUDE:

- Limited attention span and difficulty concentrating.
- With so much information to process, nervous energy abounds.

AFFIRMATIONS

- My mind is bright.
- Knowledge is power.
- I am flexible.
- I speak with confidence and clarity.

SELF-CARE RITUALS

- Begin a new book.
- Get a shoulder massage.

*Celestial
Event Calendar
Page 158*

STELLAR REFLECTIONS

What am I really curious about right now?

....

....

....

....

....

....

....

....

When my mind feels scattered, what are my go-to practices to center myself?

....

....

....

....

....

....

....

....

STELLAR REFLECTIONS

What's my unique learning style?

....

....

....

....

....

....

....

....

What language would I love to learn, and why?

....

....

....

....

....

....

....

....

....

STELLAR REFLECTIONS

If I could talk to anyone right now, it would be _____ because:

....

....

....

....

....

....

....

Here's how I define being a good communicator:

....

....

....

....

....

....

....

....

Cancer New Moon

THE OPPORTUNITIES INCLUDE:

- Honoring your emotions and letting them guide you.
- Exploring who and what help you feel more at home in the world.

THE CHALLENGES INCLUDE:

- An emphasis on the emotional may obscure the rational.
- A tendency to move in a slow and indirect manner may yield frustration.

AFFIRMATIONS

- I trust my emotions.
- I know how to take care of myself.
- I feel protected.
- I am nourished.

SELF-CARE RITUALS

- Prepare a home-cooked meal.
- Reach out to a relative.

Celestial Event Calendar Page 158

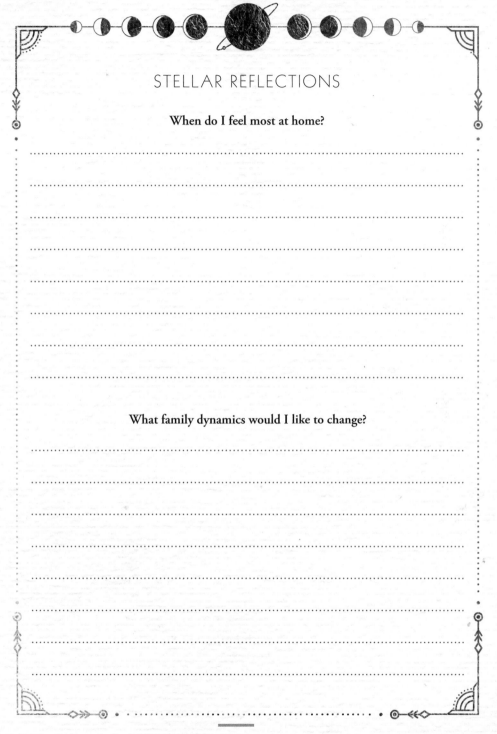

STELLAR REFLECTIONS

When do I feel most at home?

....
....
....
....
....
....
....

What family dynamics would I like to change?

....
....
....
....
....
....
....
....

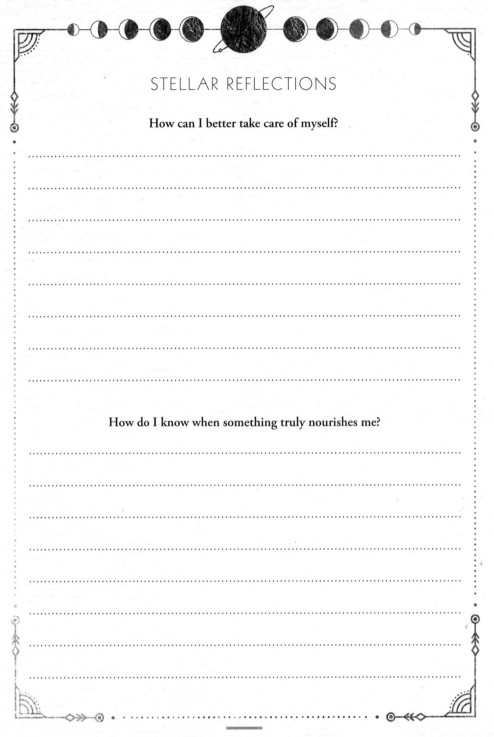

STELLAR REFLECTIONS

How can I better take care of myself?

....
....
....
....
....
....
....

How do I know when something truly nourishes me?

....
....
....
....
....
....
....

STELLAR REFLECTIONS

My definition of safety is:

....
....
....
....
....
....
....
....

A DIY home project I'd like to undertake is:

....
....
....
....
....
....
....
....

Leo New Moon

THE OPPORTUNITIES INCLUDE:

- Becoming more generous in how you express love.
- Being creative and showcasing your unique self.

THE CHALLENGES INCLUDE:

- People may be prickly, notably if their pride is wounded.
- A fear of embarrassment keeps you from sharing your talents.

AFFIRMATIONS

- My heart is a stream of love.
- Being generous makes my life richer.
- I am bold.
- I feel royal.

SELF-CARE RITUALS

- Do an artistic project.
- Spend time with a child.

Celestial Event Calendar Page 158

STELLAR REFLECTIONS

How can I invite more fun into my life?

....
....
....
....
....
....
....
....

What's standing in the way of living with a more open heart?

....
....
....
....
....
....
....
....

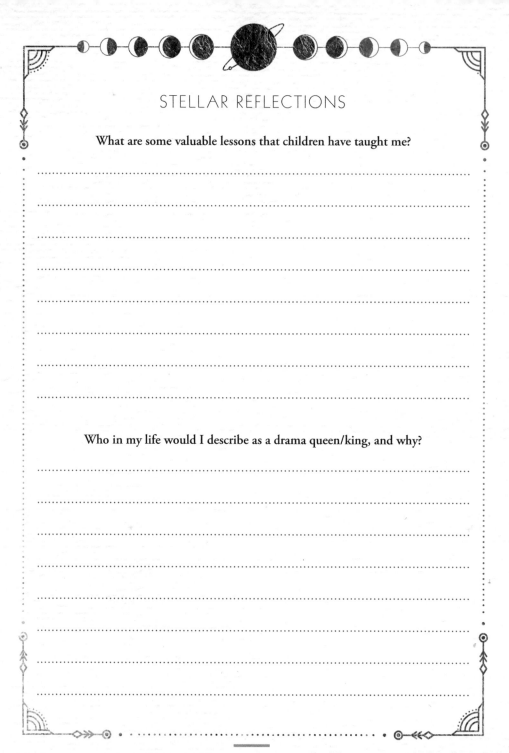

STELLAR REFLECTIONS

What are some valuable lessons that children have taught me?

....
....
....
....
....
....
....

Who in my life would I describe as a drama queen/king, and why?

....
....
....
....
....
....
....

STELLAR REFLECTIONS

My favorite pieces of art include:

....
....
....
....
....
....
....

This is what brings me deep joy:

....
....
....
....
....
....
....

Virgo New Moon

THE OPPORTUNITIES INCLUDE:

- Paying attention to the details leads to a solution.
- Finding ways to be of service to others.

THE CHALLENGES INCLUDE:

- A penchant for perfection can cause you to be more critical.
- Excess worry and anxiety can occur when things appear out of order.

AFFIRMATIONS

- I am of service.
- I am enough.
- I see the parts and I see the whole.
- Perfection is an illusion.

SELF-CARE RITUALS

- Organize your files or kitchen cabinets.
- Do a craft project.

Celestial Event Calendar Page 158

STELLAR REFLECTIONS

What realms of my life would benefit from more organization?

....
....
....
....
....
....
....
....

How can I have a critical eye without being overly critical?

....
....
....
....
....
....
....
....

STELLAR REFLECTIONS

What do I worry about most?

....

....

....

....

....

....

....

How can being more detail-oriented help me achieve my aims?

....

....

....

....

....

....

....

....

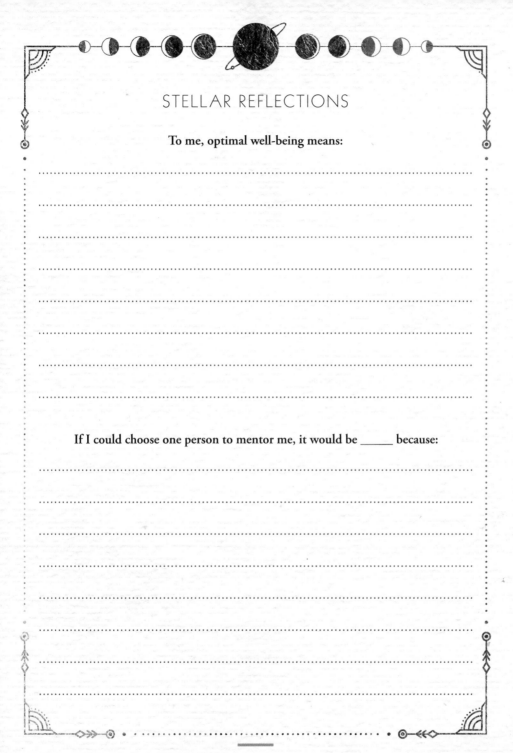

STELLAR REFLECTIONS

To me, optimal well-being means:

....

....

....

....

....

....

....

If I could choose one person to mentor me, it would be _____ because:

....

....

....

....

....

....

....

Libra New Moon

THE OPPORTUNITIES INCLUDE:

- Discovering how alliances make your life more enjoyable.
- Exploring pathways that create equitable outcomes.

THE CHALLENGES INCLUDE:

- Compromising your needs in an attempt to keep the peace.
- An aversion to making a wrong choice could lead to procrastination.

AFFIRMATIONS

- Equality is important to me.
- I trust my choices.
- I am a good ally.
- I see beauty.

SELF-CARE RITUALS

- Plan a social gathering.
- Read poetry.

Celestial
Event Calendar
Page 158

STELLAR REFLECTIONS

When I perceive that something is unjust, how does it affect me?

....

....

....

....

....

....

....

How can I invite more pleasure into my life?

....

....

....

....

....

....

....

STELLAR REFLECTIONS

What's my relationship with compromise?

....

....

....

....

....

....

....

....

What do I find utterly beautiful?

....

....

....

....

....

....

....

....

STELLAR REFLECTIONS

My definition of justice is:

....

....

....

....

....

....

....

....

....

If I were to plan a perfect date, here's what we'd do:

....

....

....

....

....

....

....

....

Scorpio New Moon

THE OPPORTUNITIES INCLUDE:

- Connecting to an unwavering commitment.
- Mining your emotions to better understand what you are feeling.

THE CHALLENGES INCLUDE:

- An all-or-nothing orientation leaves no middle ground.
- Truth may be veiled, with people assuming a more secretive stance.

AFFIRMATIONS

- Treasures reside under the surface.
- My desires run deep.
- The dark is illuminating.
- I trust my emotions.

SELF-CARE RITUALS

- Deep clean your closets.
- Practice intermittent fasting.

Celestial Event Calendar Page 158

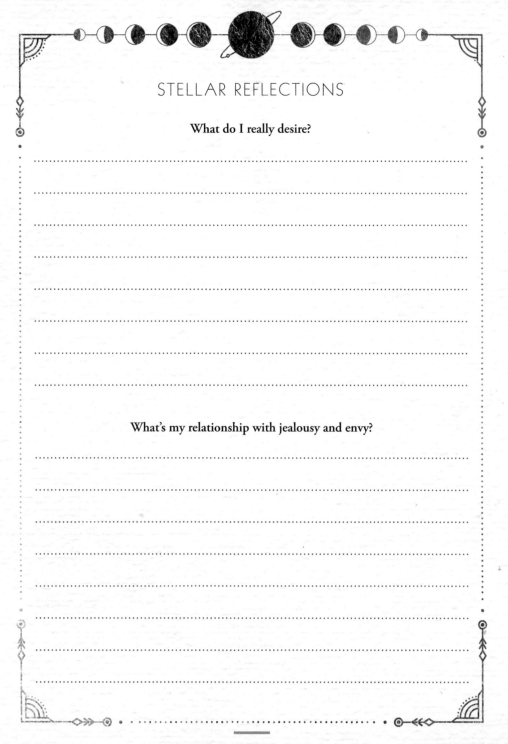

STELLAR REFLECTIONS

What do I really desire?

....
....
....
....
....
....
....
....

What's my relationship with jealousy and envy?

....
....
....
....
....
....
....
....

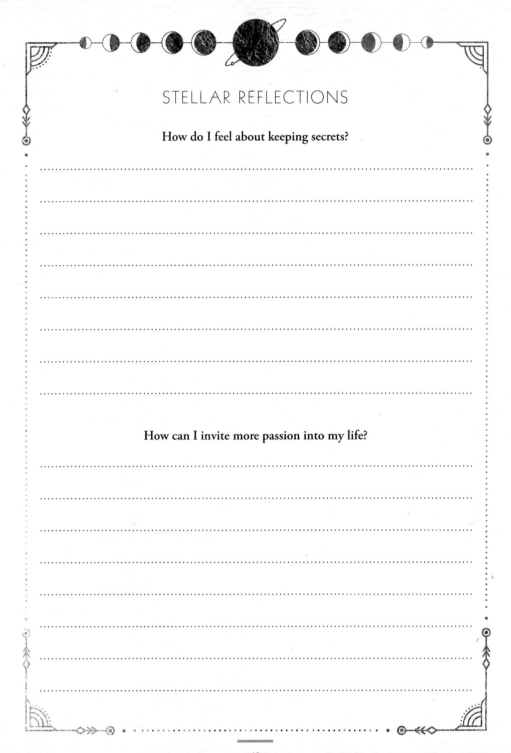

STELLAR REFLECTIONS

How do I feel about keeping secrets?

....
....
....
....
....
....
....
....
....

How can I invite more passion into my life?

....
....
....
....
....
....
....
....
....

STELLAR REFLECTIONS

Three steps I could take to feel more connected to my sexuality include:

....

....

....

....

....

....

....

The emotions that I feel the most strongly are:

....

....

....

....

....

....

....

Sagittarius New Moon

THE OPPORTUNITIES INCLUDE:

- Envisioning what you'd like your future to look like.
- Exploring philosophical or spiritual wisdom.

THE CHALLENGES INCLUDE:

- Overenthusiasm leading to exhaustion.
- An overzealous perspective may rub others the wrong way.

AFFIRMATIONS

- I give myself permission to aim high.
- I am wise.
- My vision is clear.
- I have faith.

SELF-CARE RITUALS

- Create a vision board.
- Read a travel magazine.

Celestial Event Calendar Page 158

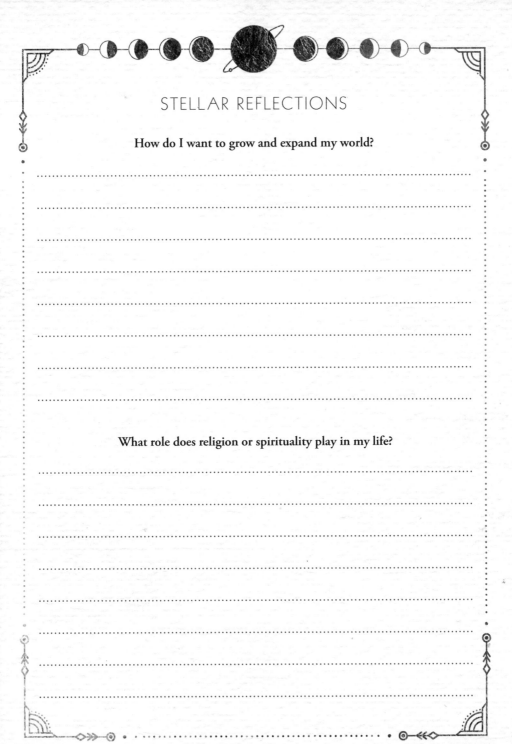

STELLAR REFLECTIONS

How do I want to grow and expand my world?

....
....
....
....
....
....
....
....

What role does religion or spirituality play in my life?

....
....
....
....
....
....
....
....

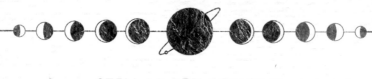

STELLAR REFLECTIONS

If I could design my ideal travel adventure, what would it be?

....
....
....
....
....
....
....

In which areas of my life would I like to take more risks?

....
....
....
....
....
....
....

STELLAR REFLECTIONS

My goals for the next few months are:

....

....

....

....

....

....

....

At the core of my beliefs are these essential tenets:

....

....

....

....

....

....

....

Capricorn New Moon

THE OPPORTUNITIES INCLUDE:

- Defining an achievement toward which you'd like to work.
- Appreciating how creating solid foundations builds lasting structures.

THE CHALLENGES INCLUDE:

- An emphasis on being dutiful may create a somber environment.
- Hard work may lead to burnout.

AFFIRMATIONS

- I am responsible.
- Success is within my reach.
- Loyalty is an asset.
- I have endurance.

SELF-CARE RITUALS

- Work on a financial budget.
- Do stretching exercises.

Celestial Event Calendar Page 158

STELLAR REFLECTIONS

What does success mean to me?

....
....
....
....
....
....
....
....

What would I like my legacy to be?

....
....
....
....
....
....
....
....

STELLAR REFLECTIONS

To what and whom am I loyal?

In what ways can I be more financially responsible?

STELLAR REFLECTIONS

The three historical figures I'd most like to get advice from include:

....

....

....

....

....

....

....

If I were to run any business, the most rewarding would be:

....

....

....

....

....

....

....

....

....

Aquarius New Moon

THE OPPORTUNITIES INCLUDE:

- Exploring how a new technology offers unique solutions.
- Investigating innovative and alternative approaches to well-being.

THE CHALLENGES INCLUDE:

- An emphasis on the rational that doesn't consider the emotional.
- Sacrificing your personal needs to support those of a group.

AFFIRMATIONS

- I am a citizen of the world.
- Collectives have power.
- I sense subtle energies.
- I can help make a difference.

SELF-CARE RITUALS

- Meditate with crystals.
- Do a community project.

Celestial Event Calendar Page 158

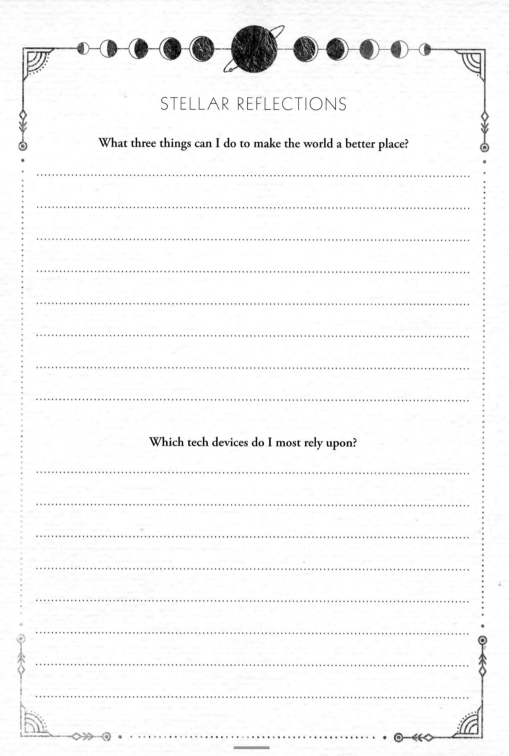

STELLAR REFLECTIONS

What three things can I do to make the world a better place?

....
....
....
....
....
....
....
....

Which tech devices do I most rely upon?

....
....
....
....
....
....
....
....

STELLAR REFLECTIONS

Which communities or groups align with my vision and values?

....
....
....
....
....
....
....

In what ways do I march to the beat of my own drum?

....
....
....
....
....
....

STELLAR REFLECTIONS

My ideal future would look like this:

....

....

....

....

....

....

....

....

These are the areas of my life in which I wish I had more freedom:

....

....

....

....

....

....

....

....

Pisces New Moon

THE OPPORTUNITIES INCLUDE:

- Connecting to a more soulful way of perceiving life.
- Being more empathetic and compassionate.

THE CHALLENGES INCLUDE:

- An oversensitivity to others can lead to blurred boundaries.
- Greater difficulty in discerning what's truly real from what you want to be real.

AFFIRMATIONS

- Dreams can come true.
- We are all connected.
- I am love.
- I am loved.

SELF-CARE RITUALS

- Take a bath.
- Make art.

Celestial
Event Calendar
Page 158

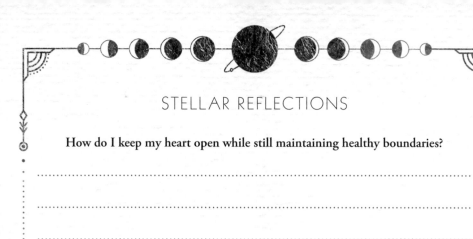

STELLAR REFLECTIONS

How do I keep my heart open while still maintaining healthy boundaries?

....
....
....
....
....
....
....

What's keeping me from showering myself with love?

....
....
....
....
....
....
....
....

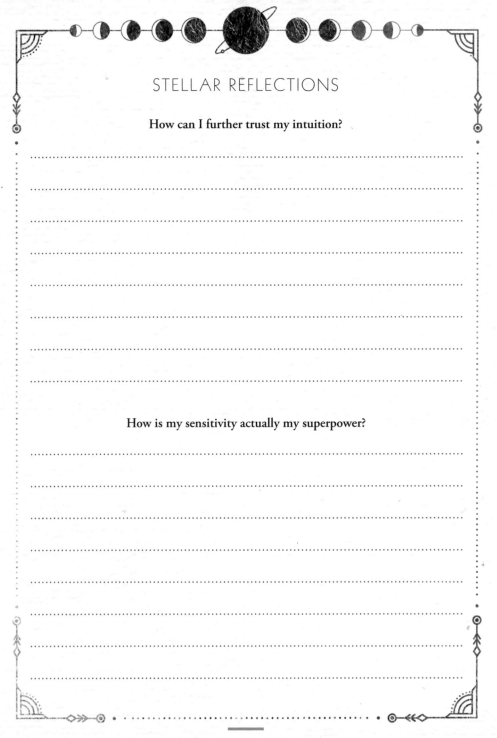

STELLAR REFLECTIONS

How can I further trust my intuition?

....

....

....

....

....

....

....

How is my sensitivity actually my superpower?

....

....

....

....

....

....

....

STELLAR REFLECTIONS

These three people truly inspire me:

If I were living my dream life, it would look like this:

Aries Full Moon

THE OPPORTUNITIES INCLUDE:

- Discovering the will to go the extra mile for someone.
- Being a champion for beauty, justice, and peace.

THE CHALLENGES INCLUDE:

- Having little patience when perceiving that something is unfair.
- The possibility of a divide between what's best for you and what's best for a relationship.

AFFIRMATIONS

- I fight for justice.
- My will is strong.
- I deserve pleasure.
- I am a good friend.

SELF-CARE RITUALS

- Give yourself a facial.
- Exercise with a friend.

Celestial Event Calendar Page 158

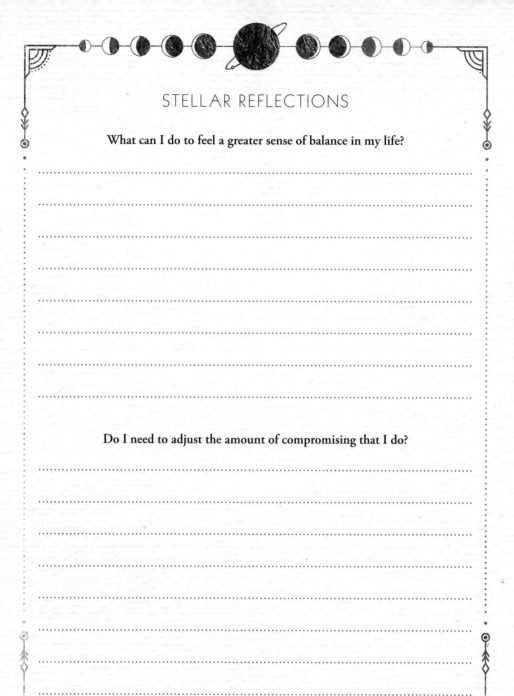

STELLAR REFLECTIONS

What can I do to feel a greater sense of balance in my life?

....

....

....

....

....

....

....

Do I need to adjust the amount of compromising that I do?

....

....

....

....

....

....

....

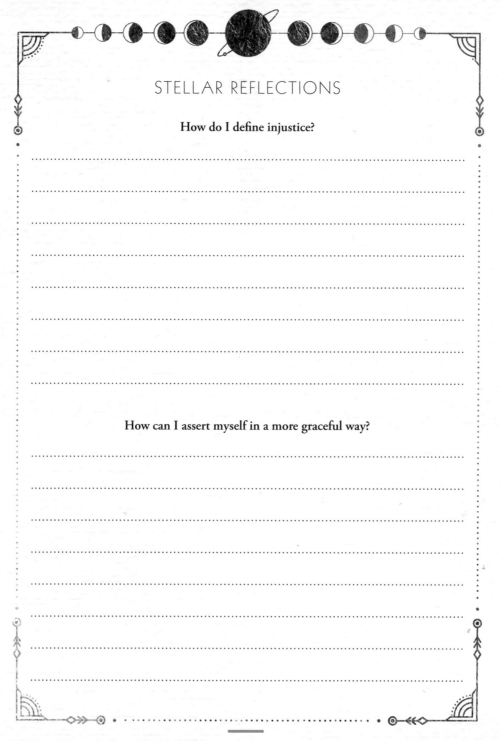

STELLAR REFLECTIONS

How do I define injustice?

....

....

....

....

....

....

....

....

How can I assert myself in a more graceful way?

....

....

....

....

....

....

....

....

STELLAR REFLECTIONS

Three ways that I can invite more beauty and pleasure into my life are:

....

....

....

....

....

....

....

....

My friends who I would describe as really courageous include:

....

....

....

....

....

....

....

Taurus Full Moon

THE OPPORTUNITIES INCLUDE:

- Feeling nourished by sensual experiences.
- Seeing how practical solutions yield transformative outcomes.

THE CHALLENGES INCLUDE:

- A lack of flexibility may restrict options.
- Feeling resistant to staying with powerful emotions.

AFFIRMATIONS

- I am safe and secure.
- I can manifest.
- My sensuality nurtures me.
- My beauty runs deep.

SELF-CARE RITUALS

- Do a mud mask.
- Exfoliate your skin.

Celestial Event Calendar Page 158

STELLAR REFLECTIONS

How can I feel more rooted and secure?

....
....
....
....
....
....
....

How can I give more voice to my passions?

....
....
....
....
....
....
....

STELLAR REFLECTIONS

How do I know when something really feels good to me?

....
....
....
....
....
....
....
....

How can being practical help me feel more empowered?

....
....
....
....
....
....
....
....

STELLAR REFLECTIONS

The people that I trust with my deepest secrets are:

....

....

....

....

....

....

....

Ways to bring more sensual pleasure into my life include:

....

....

....

....

....

....

....

Gemini Full Moon

THE OPPORTUNITIES INCLUDE:

- Gathering more data to bolster your message.
- Discovering the difference between wisdom and knowledge.

THE CHALLENGES INCLUDE:

- Second-guessing what you believe to be true.
- Dealing with an excess of information may rev up your nervous system.

AFFIRMATIONS

- I know how to know.
- Options are to be explored.
- Curiosity leads to understanding.
- Being versatile yields opportunities.

SELF-CARE RITUALS

- Do breathing exercises.
- Research a wellness modality.

Celestial Event Calendar Page 158

STELLAR REFLECTIONS

How do I know when something is true?

....
....
....
....
....
....
....
....

What's my go-to resource for gathering new information?

....
....
....
....
....
....
....
....

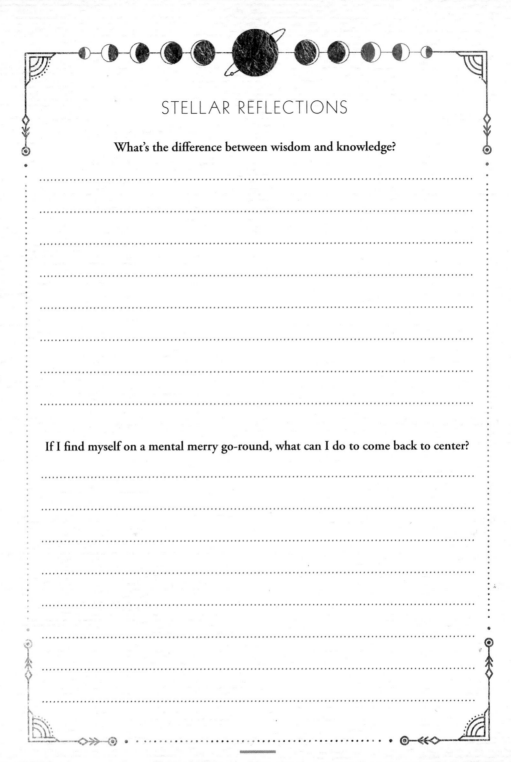

STELLAR REFLECTIONS

What's the difference between wisdom and knowledge?

If I find myself on a mental merry go-round, what can I do to come back to center?

STELLAR REFLECTIONS

My three most fervent beliefs are:

....

....

....

....

....

....

....

....

These people have taught me so much about life:

....

....

....

....

....

....

....

Cancer Full Moon

THE OPPORTUNITIES INCLUDE:

- Learning how to nourish yourself and others more efficiently.
- Making your workplace feel more homey.

THE CHALLENGES INCLUDE:

- Emotionality may undermine authority.
- Feeling the need to attend to a flurry of responsibilities.

AFFIRMATIONS

- Being responsible nurtures me.
- I have a duty to protect myself.
- I trust my feelings.
- My roots are strong.

SELF-CARE RITUALS

- Clean out your pantry.
- Look through old photos.

Celestial Event Calendar Page 158

STELLAR REFLECTIONS

What people, places, and things make me feel the most at home?

....

....

....

....

....

....

....

....

How can I further show my family how important my work is to me?

....

....

....

....

....

....

....

....

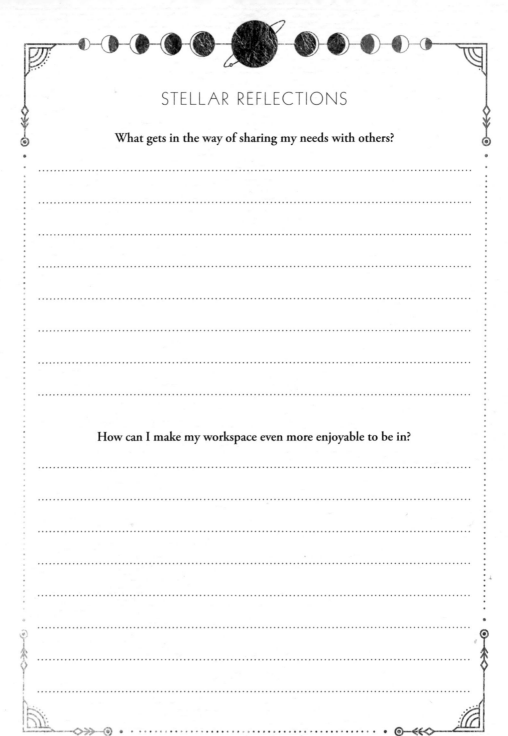

STELLAR REFLECTIONS

What gets in the way of sharing my needs with others?

....

....

....

....

....

....

....

How can I make my workspace even more enjoyable to be in?

....

....

....

....

....

....

....

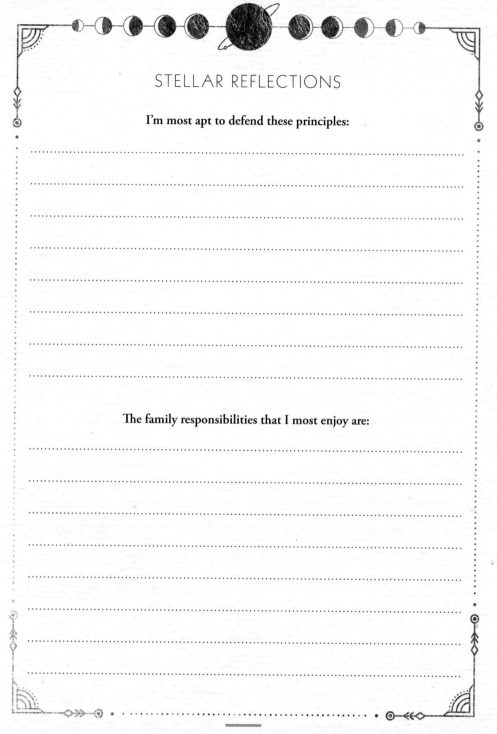

STELLAR REFLECTIONS

I'm most apt to defend these principles:

....

....

....

....

....

....

....

The family responsibilities that I most enjoy are:

....

....

....

....

....

....

....

Leo Full Moon

THE OPPORTUNITIES INCLUDE:

- Adopting a childlike perspective can create a revolutionary solution.
- Seeing how being authentically yourself helps others.

THE CHALLENGES INCLUDE:

- Being too self-focused may disrupt group dynamics.
- Pomp and circumstance obscure scientific facts.

AFFIRMATIONS

- It's important to make space for everyone.
- I contribute in a unique way.
- I love my inner child.
- I am creative.

SELF-CARE RITUALS

- Write a letter to your inner child.
- Give yourself a scalp massage.

Celestial Event Calendar Page 158

STELLAR REFLECTIONS

What's my unique contribution to humanity?

....

....

....

....

....

....

....

Where have I seen generosity be a key to success?

....

....

....

....

....

....

....

STELLAR REFLECTIONS

Do I give myself as much space and freedom as I need?

....
....
....
....
....
....
....

If I were to commit to one creative project this year, what would it be?

....
....
....
....
....
....
....

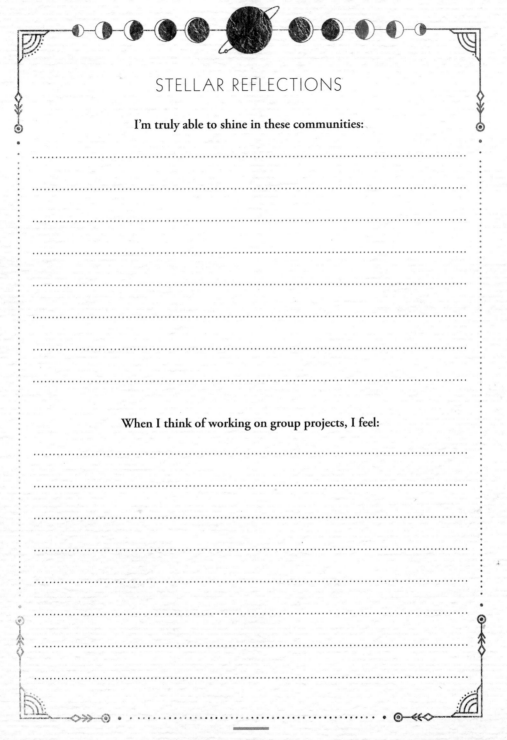

STELLAR REFLECTIONS

I'm truly able to shine in these communities:

....

....

....

....

....

....

....

....

When I think of working on group projects, I feel:

....

....

....

....

....

....

....

....

Virgo Full Moon

THE OPPORTUNITIES INCLUDE:

- Perceiving how mind, body, and spirit are woven together leads to healing.
- Seeing the differences as well as the similarities.

THE CHALLENGES INCLUDE:

- Confusing service with sacrifice.
- Perfectionism leading to procrastination.

AFFIRMATIONS

- I am of service.
- Healing is my birthright.
- The parts make the whole.
- My perceptive skills are strong.

SELF-CARE RITUALS

- Decode a recent dream.
- Paint with watercolors.

Celestial
Event Calendar
Page 158

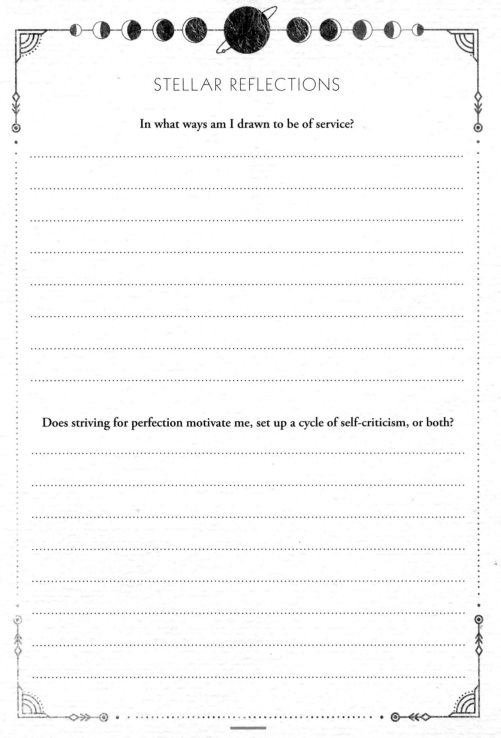

STELLAR REFLECTIONS

In what ways am I drawn to be of service?

....
....
....
....
....
....
....
....

Does striving for perfection motivate me, set up a cycle of self-criticism, or both?

....
....
....
....
....
....
....
....

STELLAR REFLECTIONS

How can I better organize my days to create more ease?

....
....
....
....
....
....
....
....

How can I approach situations both rationally and intuitively?

....
....
....
....
....
....
....
....

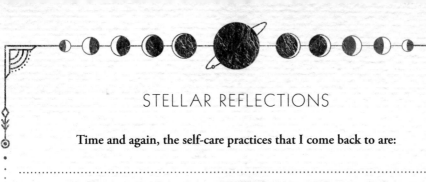

STELLAR REFLECTIONS

Time and again, the self-care practices that I come back to are:

....

....

....

....

....

....

....

I define holistic well-being as:

....

....

....

....

....

....

Libra Full Moon

THE OPPORTUNITIES INCLUDE:

- Forging alliances can help you pursue your desires.
- Using a diplomatic strategy aids in better championing an important cause.

THE CHALLENGES INCLUDE:

- A propensity for compromise may stifle the pursuit of your aims.
- A partner's needs can cause you to feel overshadowed.

AFFIRMATIONS

- Justice ignites my soul.
- My value is strong.
- I am a good partner.
- I appreciate my own beauty.

SELF-CARE RITUALS

- Surround yourself with art.
- Hang out with a friend.

Celestial Event Calendar Page 158

STELLAR REFLECTIONS

How can I fight for a relationship while not neglecting my personal needs?

....

....

....

....

....

....

....

How can I catalyze more beauty in my life?

....

....

....

....

....

....

....

STELLAR REFLECTIONS

Do I compromise too much, not enough, or just enough?

How can my partnership better meet my needs?

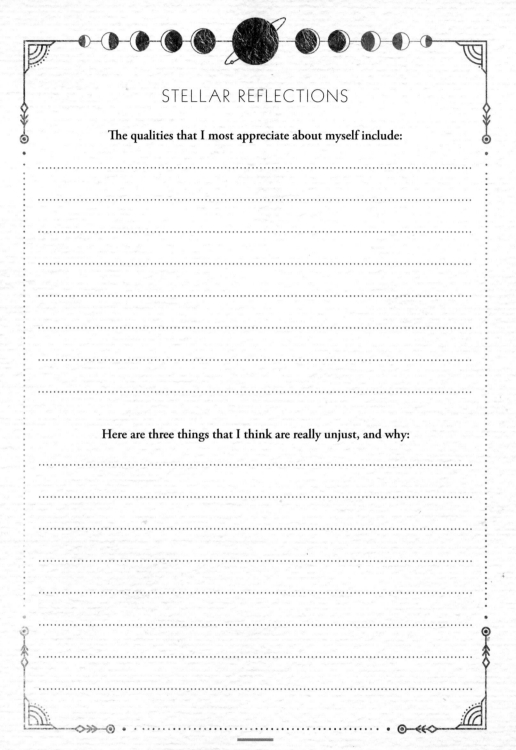

STELLAR REFLECTIONS

The qualities that I most appreciate about myself include:

....

....

....

....

....

....

....

....

Here are three things that I think are really unjust, and why:

....

....

....

....

....

....

....

....

Scorpio Full Moon

THE OPPORTUNITIES INCLUDE:

- Seeing how a tenacious approach helps override obstacles.
- Having a powerful sexual experience.

THE CHALLENGES INCLUDE:

- Feeling torn between wanting change and wanting things to stay the same.
- Experiencing uncertainty about whether to take things at face value.

AFFIRMATIONS

- I trust my core instincts.
- Treasures reside below the surface.
- I own my power.
- I am resilient.

SELF-CARE RITUALS

- Read something erotic.
- Explore a mysterious subject.

Celestial Event Calendar Page 158

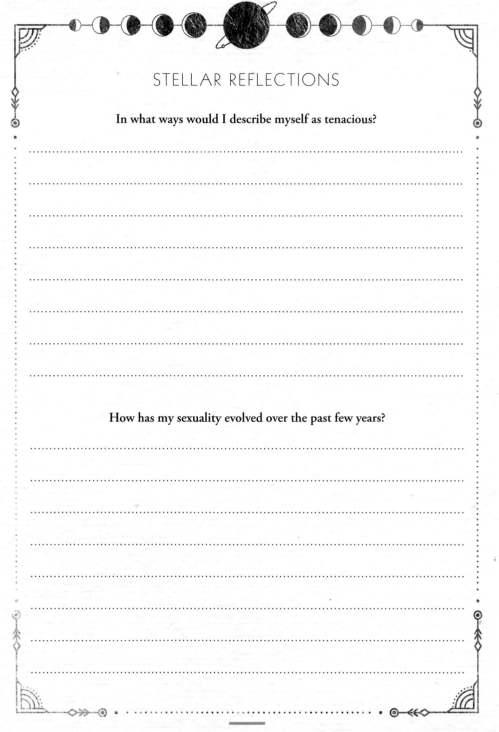

STELLAR REFLECTIONS

In what ways would I describe myself as tenacious?

....

....

....

....

....

....

....

....

How has my sexuality evolved over the past few years?

....

....

....

....

....

....

....

....

STELLAR REFLECTIONS

How apt am I to dig below the surface when dealing with practical matters?

....
....
....
....
....
....
....
....

How can I transform my relationship with money?

....
....
....
....
....
....
....
....

STELLAR REFLECTIONS

When things are really intense, I feel:

....

....

....

....

....

....

....

I would feel empowered if I could share this secret with someone:

....

....

....

....

....

....

....

Sagittarius Full Moon

THE OPPORTUNITIES INCLUDE:

- Stepping back allows you to see the bigger picture.
- Expanding your understanding of what's possible.

THE CHALLENGES INCLUDE:

- Selectively using facts to push forth your agenda.
- Overstimulation causes nervous exhaustion.

AFFIRMATIONS

- I'm optimistic I will find the answer.
- Many things are possible.
- Discovery inspires me.
- I am hopeful.

SELF-CARE RITUALS

- Meditate by candlelight.
- Take a long walk.

Celestial Event Calendar Page 158

STELLAR REFLECTIONS

If my life were a novel, what would its title be?

....

....

....

....

....

....

....

If I could travel anywhere, where would I go and what would I want to discover?

....

....

....

....

....

....

....

....

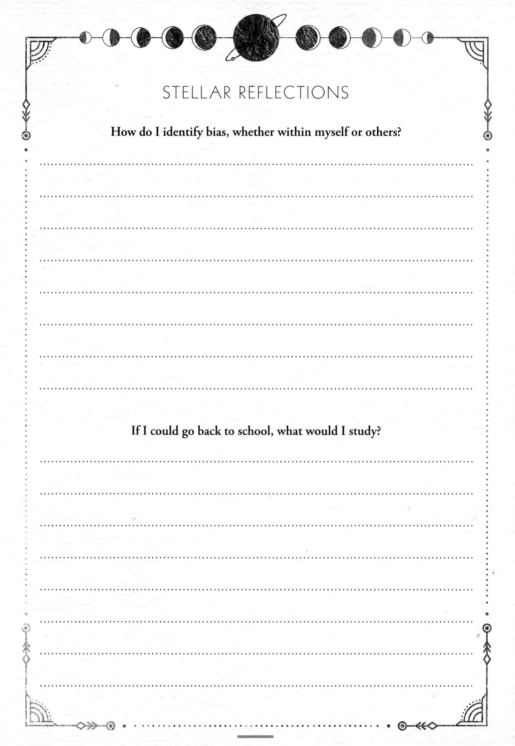

STELLAR REFLECTIONS

How do I identify bias, whether within myself or others?

....

....

....

....

....

....

....

If I could go back to school, what would I study?

....

....

....

....

....

....

....

STELLAR REFLECTIONS

Here's how my beliefs have changed over the years:

....
....
....
....
....
....
....
....
....
....

The country, culture, or subject matter I am interested in exploring next is:

....
....
....
....
....
....
....
....
....
....

Capricorn Full Moon

THE OPPORTUNITIES INCLUDE:

- Mastering the rules can yield a feeling of protection.
- Proceeding slowly feels very nourishing.

THE CHALLENGES INCLUDE:

- Loyalties being called into question.
- Feeling uncertain whether to take a direct or an indirect route.

AFFIRMATIONS

- I am responsible for my emotions.
- Time is on my side.
- My home nurtures me.
- I feel grounded.

SELF-CARE RITUALS

- Plan family activities.
- Read about your ancestry.

Celestial Event Calendar Page 158

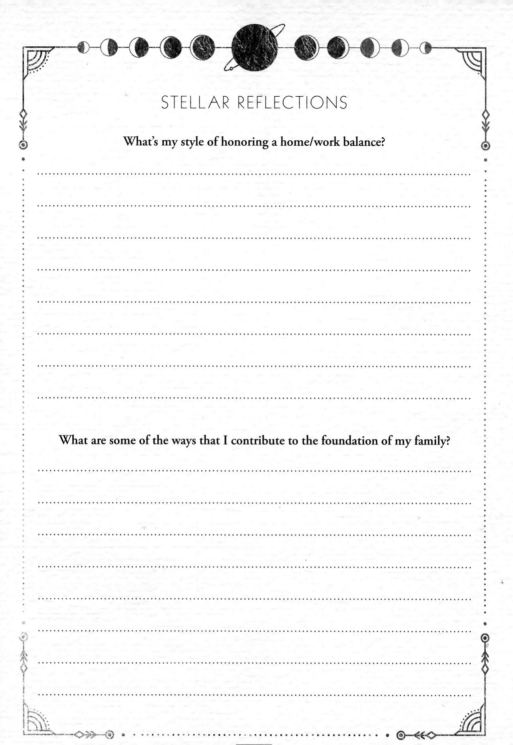

STELLAR REFLECTIONS

What's my style of honoring a home/work balance?

....

....

....

....

....

....

....

What are some of the ways that I contribute to the foundation of my family?

....

....

....

....

....

....

....

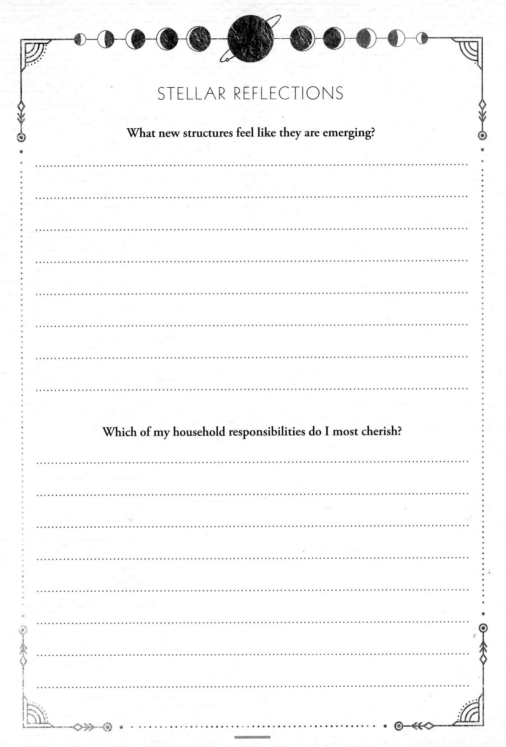

STELLAR REFLECTIONS

What new structures feel like they are emerging?

....

....

....

....

....

....

....

Which of my household responsibilities do I most cherish?

....

....

....

....

....

....

....

....

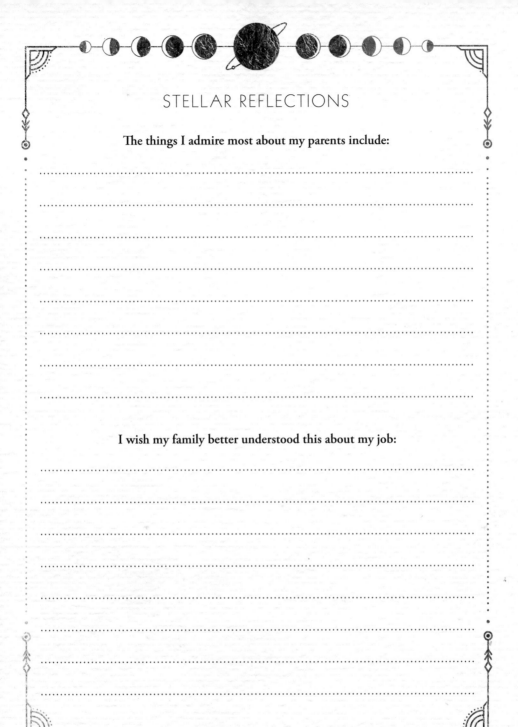

STELLAR REFLECTIONS

The things I admire most about my parents include:

....

....

....

....

....

....

....

....

I wish my family better understood this about my job:

....

....

....

....

....

....

....

....

Aquarius Full Moon

THE OPPORTUNITIES INCLUDE:

- You are inspired by art that promotes social causes.
- You discover technology that connects you to your creativity.

THE CHALLENGES INCLUDE:

- There is tension between the needs of an organization and those of its members.
- An overly intellectual approach can limit creative expression.

AFFIRMATIONS

- I give voice to innovative solutions.
- I see the beauty of connections.
- The future is bright.
- I'm a creative thinker.

SELF-CARE RITUALS

- Participate in a group art project.
- Research health apps.

Celestial Event Calendar Page 158

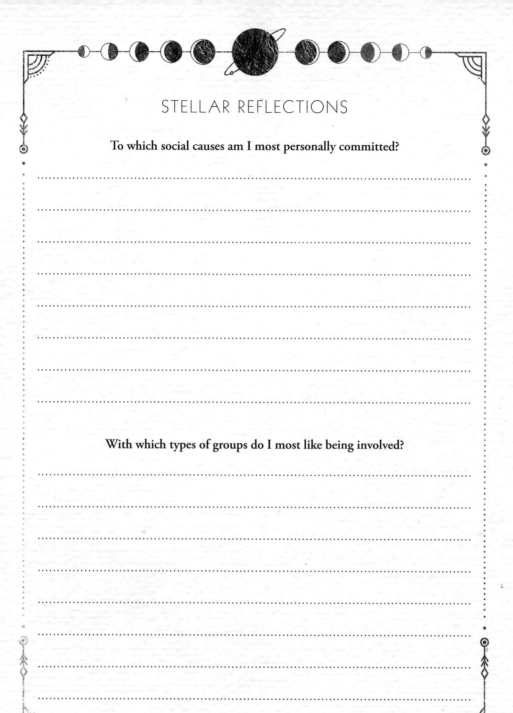

STELLAR REFLECTIONS

To which social causes am I most personally committed?

....

....

....

....

....

....

....

....

With which types of groups do I most like being involved?

....

....

....

....

....

....

....

....

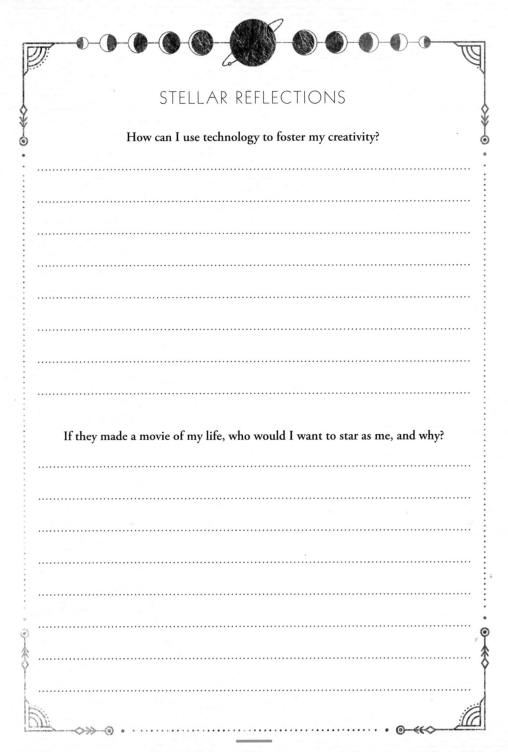

STELLAR REFLECTIONS

How can I use technology to foster my creativity?

....

....

....

....

....

....

....

....

If they made a movie of my life, who would I want to star as me, and why?

....

....

....

....

....

....

....

....

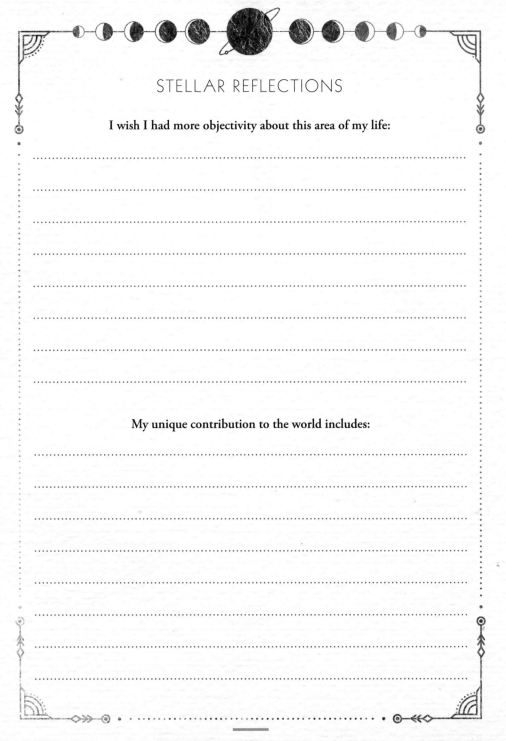

STELLAR REFLECTIONS

I wish I had more objectivity about this area of my life:

....

....

....

....

....

....

....

My unique contribution to the world includes:

....

....

....

....

....

....

....

Pisces Full Moon

THE OPPORTUNITIES INCLUDE:

- Learning new techniques to bolster your intuition.
- Realizing that forgiveness leads to healing.

THE CHALLENGES INCLUDE:

- A wandering mind may have you miss some important details.
- Striving for perfection can derail progress.

AFFIRMATIONS

- I am love.
- My intuition is strong.
- Forgiveness heals.
- My dreams inspire me.

SELF-CARE RITUALS

- Take photographs.
- Forgive someone.

Celestial Event Calendar Page 158

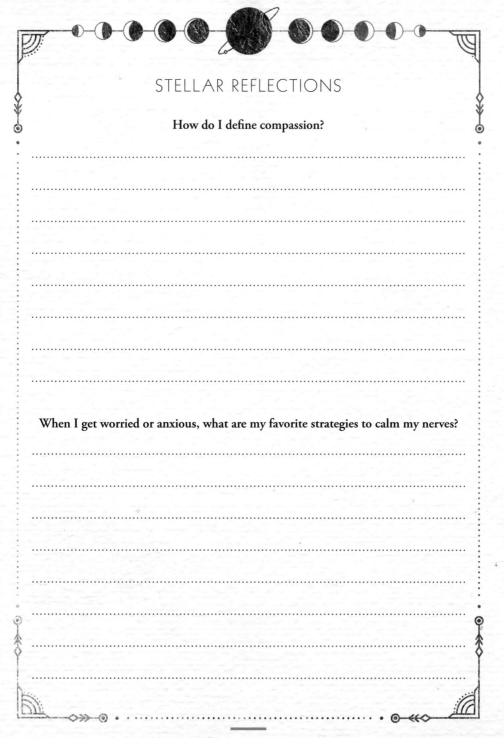

STELLAR REFLECTIONS

How do I define compassion?

....
....
....
....
....
....
....

When I get worried or anxious, what are my favorite strategies to calm my nerves?

....
....
....
....
....
....
....
....

STELLAR REFLECTIONS

How do I connect to my inner muse?

....

....

....

....

....

....

....

What can I let go of that is no longer serving me?

....

....

....

....

....

....

....

STELLAR REFLECTIONS

Three things for which I am really grateful are:

....

....

....

....

....

....

....

I forgive myself for:

....

....

....

....

....

....

....

PLANETARY
RETROGRADES

When a planet is in retrograde motion, it appears—from our perspective on Earth—to be traveling backward across the skyscape. When the planets Mercury, Venus, and Mars are in retrograde, we are given the invitation for do-overs, learning from the past, and capturing new insights that can help us build a more complete understanding of ourselves and our place in the world. In the following sections, you'll discover perspectives and journaling questions that will help you make the most of these planetary retrograde periods.

Mercury Retrograde

WHEN DOES IT OCCUR?

Mercury Retrograde lasts approximately three weeks and occurs about three times a year.

OPPORTUNITIES FOR AWARENESS

Experiences we have during Mercury Retrograde may lead to:

- Finding new sources through which we can access information.
- Discovering alternative routes to get us to our chosen destination.
- Removing obstacles that restrict our communicating with ease.
- Placing a greater value on our intuition.

STRATEGIES TO SIDESTEP STRESS

Minimize Mercury Retrograde challenges by employing these approaches:

- Ensure your tech devices and transport vehicles are in good working order.
- Finish your to-do list before attempting new projects.
- Be slow and thoughtful in communication.
- Double-check details of your travel itinerary.

SELF-CARE RITUALS

- Re-read a favorite book.
- Take a break from social media.

Celestial Event Calendar Page 158

STELLAR REFLECTIONS

What do I need so that I can further trust my intuition?

....
....
....
....
....
....
....
....

Who from my past can help me solve a current problem I'm encountering?

....
....
....
....
....
....
....
....

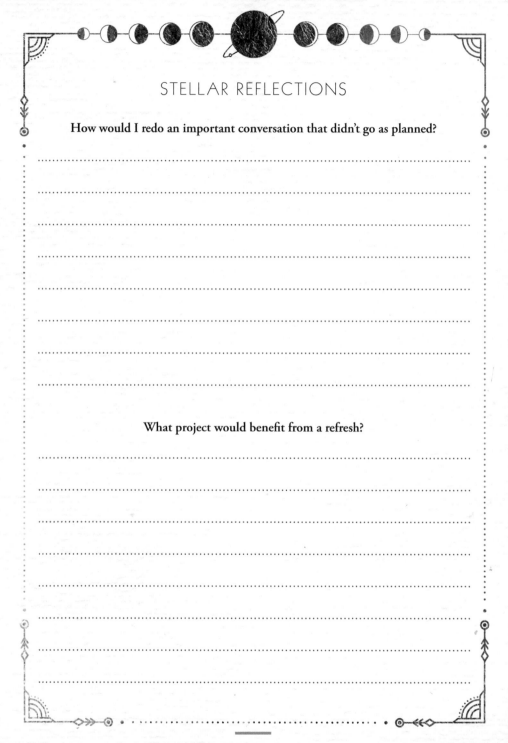

STELLAR REFLECTIONS

How would I redo an important conversation that didn't go as planned?

....
....
....
....
....
....
....
....

What project would benefit from a refresh?

....
....
....
....
....
....
....

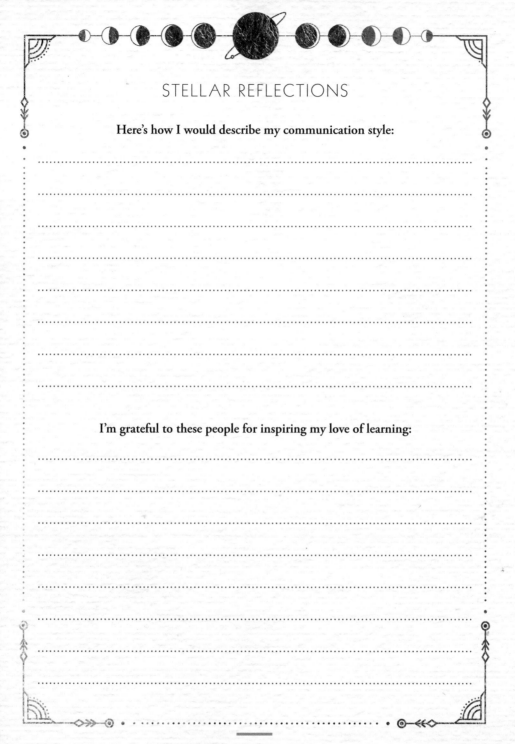

STELLAR REFLECTIONS

Here's how I would describe my communication style:

....
....
....
....
....
....
....
....

I'm grateful to these people for inspiring my love of learning:

....
....
....
....
....
....
....

Venus Retrograde

WHEN DOES IT OCCUR?

Venus Retrograde lasts approximately six weeks and occurs about every eighteen months.

OPPORTUNITIES FOR AWARENESS

Experiences we have during Venus Retrograde may lead to:

- Further understanding what brings us pleasure.
- Discovering ways relationships can offer us more rewards.
- Honing our ability to manage our finances.
- Re-evaluating what we value.

STRATEGIES TO SIDESTEP STRESS

Minimize Venus Retrograde challenges by employing these approaches:

- Don't rush to conclusions regarding a relationship.
- Watch your potential to romanticize someone or something.
- Be mindful of how much you compromise.
- Consciously consider whether something has true value.

SELF-CARE RITUALS

- Reach out to a friend you haven't spoken to in a while.
- Take a look at your finances.

Celestial Event Calendar Page 158

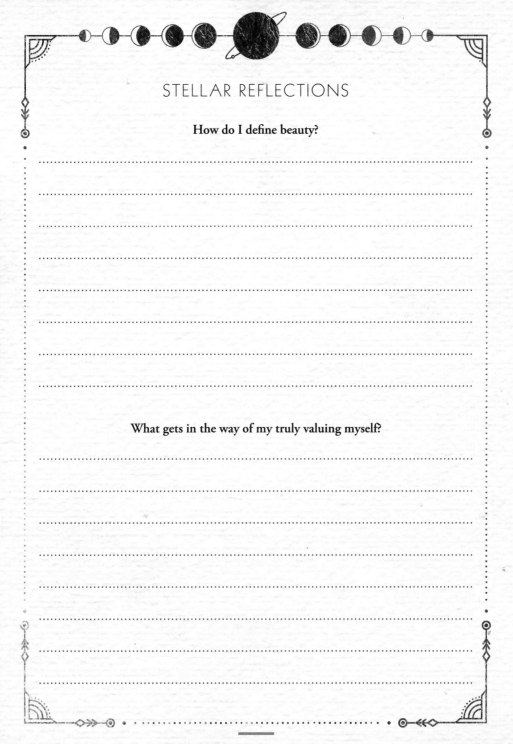

STELLAR REFLECTIONS

How do I define beauty?

....

....

....

....

....

....

....

What gets in the way of my truly valuing myself?

....

....

....

....

....

....

....

....

STELLAR REFLECTIONS

How can my relationships be even more fulfilling?

....

....

....

....

....

....

....

What does it mean to have a "rich life"?

....

....

....

....

....

....

....

....

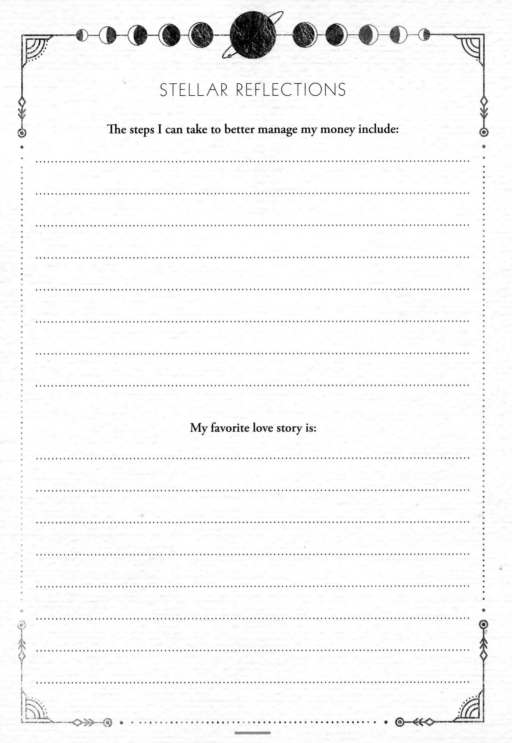

STELLAR REFLECTIONS

The steps I can take to better manage my money include:

....

....

....

....

....

....

....

My favorite love story is:

....

....

....

....

....

....

....

Mars Retrograde

WHEN DOES IT OCCUR?

Mars Retrograde lasts roughly ten weeks and occurs about every twenty-six months.

OPPORTUNITIES FOR AWARENESS

Experiences we have during Mars Retrograde may lead to:

- Clarifying just what it is that we desire.
- Seeing how to use our energy more efficiently.
- Relating more consciously to our anger.
- Becoming better at handling conflict.

STRATEGIES TO SIDESTEP STRESS

Minimize Mars Retrograde challenges by employing these approaches:

- Avoid shortcuts.
- Watch out for bouts of impatience.
- Be aware of the impact of having a very short fuse.
- Move as slowly and mindfully as possible.

SELF-CARE RITUALS

- Learn some self-defense moves.
- End your shower with a blast of cold water.

Celestial Event Calendar Page 158

STELLAR REFLECTIONS

What's my usual response when I'm confronted with fear: fight, flight, or freeze?

....
....
....
....
....
....
....
....

What's my relationship with anger?

....
....
....
....
....
....
....
....
....

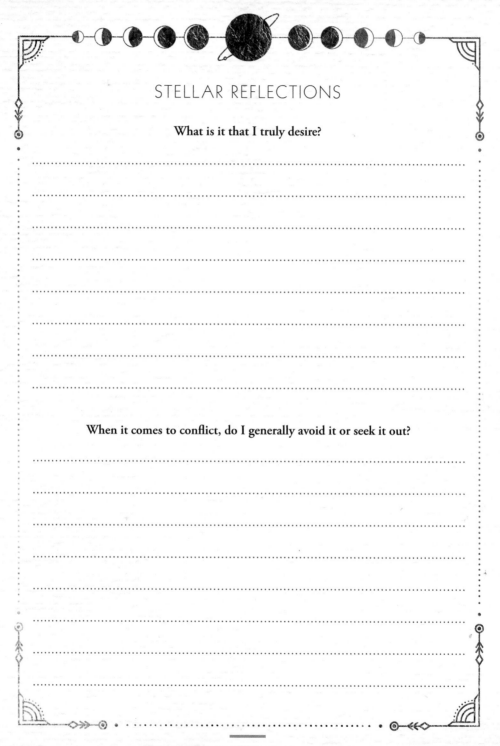

STELLAR REFLECTIONS

What is it that I truly desire?

....

....

....

....

....

....

....

When it comes to conflict, do I generally avoid it or seek it out?

....

....

....

....

....

....

....

STELLAR REFLECTIONS

Here's what I find really frustrating:

....

....

....

....

....

....

....

....

....

....

If I could strengthen my willpower, here's what I could achieve:

....

....

....

....

....

....

....

....

....

....

PLANETARY STATIONS

In addition to Mercury, Venus, and Mars, the other planets also experience retrograde cycles. Yet, since their reverse traverse lasts so long each year—four to five-plus months—we don't need to adopt special self-care considerations for the entire retrograde period but rather their planetary stations: these are the several days before and after the planet begins or ends its retrograde period. During these biannual stations, the planet's astrological invitations feel very prominent in the collective; as such, aligning our self-care strategies with the planetary stations can be quite a stellar approach to wellness.

Jupiter Station

Occurs two times a year, when Jupiter—the planet that represents wisdom, expansion, and faith—begins and ends its retrograde cycle.

ALIGN WITH THE TIMES

- Be more positive.
- Have more faith.
- Take a philosophical perspective.
- Consider a new goal.
- Tune in to your higher self.
- Look for undiscovered opportunities.
- Watch a tendency for excess.

AFFIRMATIONS

- I have faith.
- I am wise.
- Opportunities abound.

SELF-CARE RITUALS

- Create a vision board.
- Practice creative visualization.
- Drink warm lemon water in the morning.
- Use angelica flower essence.

Celestial Event Calendar Page 158

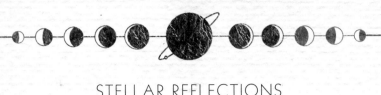

STELLAR REFLECTIONS

_____ is my role model for living life with positivity and enthusiasm because:

....

....

....

....

....

....

A recent experience that made me feel more optimistic about life was:

....

....

....

....

....

....

The three things that I most believe to be true are:

....

....

....

....

....

Saturn Station

Occurs two times a year, when Saturn—the planet that represents limits, time, and responsibility—begins and ends its retrograde cycle.

ALIGN WITH THE TIMES

- Practice discipline.
- Don't cut corners.
- Go slow and don't rush.
- Focus on the foundations.
- Dot your i's and cross your t's.
- Dedicate yourself to practices that take commitment.
- Remember that time is an important ingredient in every recipe.

AFFIRMATIONS

- I am strong.
- I am responsible.
- I achieve what I set my mind to.

SELF-CARE RITUALS

- Eat lots of leafy greens.
- Get out in nature.
- Do a yin yoga practice.
- Use gentian flower essence.

Celestial Event Calendar Page 158

STELLAR REFLECTIONS

What is it that I truly stand for?

....

....

....

....

....

What steps can I take to become a greater authority in my field?

....

....

....

....

To me, the definition of integrity is:

....

....

....

....

....

Uranus Station

Occurs two times a year, when Uranus—the planet that represents innovation, detours, and rebellions—begins and ends its retrograde cycle.

ALIGN WITH THE TIMES

- Learn to pivot more readily.
- See how chaos can breed creativity.
- Shake things up.
- Express your independence.
- Expect the unexpected.
- Let yourself be surprised.
- Remember that breakdowns can lead to breakthroughs.

AFFIRMATIONS

- I am resilient.
- I am innovative.
- I am adaptable.

SELF-CARE RITUALS

- Practice tai chi or qigong.
- Take an Epsom salt bath.
- Meditate with crystals.
- Use yarrow flower essence.

Celestial Event Calendar Page 158

STELLAR REFLECTIONS

This is what freedom means to me:

....

....

....

....

Some ways that I am unique include:

....

....

....

....

When things feel chaotic, here's what I do to feel more centered:

....

....

....

Neptune Station

Occurs two times a year, when Neptune—the planet that represents spirituality, interconnectedness, and the imagination—begins and ends its retrograde cycle.

ALIGN WITH THE TIMES

- Watch your boundaries.
- Tap into your intuition.
- Listen to your dreams.
- Go with the flow.
- Be inspired.
- Connect to your compassionate nature.
- Spend time with art.

AFFIRMATIONS

- I know love.
- We are all connected.
- I care deeply.

SELF-CARE RITUALS

- Write down your dreams.
- Get a foot massage.
- Meditate.
- Use aspen flower essence.

Celestial Event Calendar Page 158

STELLAR REFLECTIONS

How can I further trust my intuition to direct me toward the right path?

....

....

....

....

....

How does it feel when I'm going with the flow?

....

....

....

....

....

How can I be of greater service to others?

....

....

....

....

....

Pluto Station

Occurs two times a year, when Pluto—the planet that represents survival instincts, power, and transformation—begins and ends its retrograde cycle.

ALIGN WITH THE TIMES

- Solve a mystery.
- Unearth a hidden treasure.
- Tap into your power.
- Allow for surrender.
- Be honest about your unconscious motivations.
- Embrace your shadow.
- Own your desires.

AFFIRMATIONS

- Endings precede beginnings.
- My life is rich.
- My power lives in my choices.

SELF-CARE RITUALS

- Do a mini fast.
- Clean your closets.
- Apply a detoxifying facial mask.
- Use cherry plum flower essence.

Celestial Event Calendar Page 158

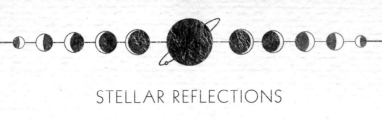

STELLAR REFLECTIONS

If I were to be honest with that someone special, here's what I would share:

....
....
....
....
....

This is my greatest fear:

....
....
....
....

To me, being in my power means:

....
....
....
....

ZODIAC SIGNS

How do you navigate the maze of self-care options available to curate a wellness strategy that mirrors your individual needs? A great place to start is with your astrology chart. The following twelve sections give you tips and Stellar Reflections tailored to the cosmic health profiles associated with each zodiac sign. Reading the section associated with your Sun sign—and those of your Moon and Ascendant signs if you know them—and answering the prompts will help you better recognize your unique strengths and stressors, and the lifestyle strategies and remedies that can support and sustain your well-being.

Aries

CHARACTERISTICS: Assertive, brave, carefree, direct, energetic, enterprising, hot-tempered, impatient, impulsive, individualistic, pioneering, willful

PERSONAL HEALTH PROFILE: Aries are blessed with great vitality. After all, yours is the first sign of the zodiac, reflecting the burgeoning of new life. Your tremendous energy reserves, fiery spirit, and pioneering nature are qualities that can help you be a champion for your well-being.

WELLNESS THERAPIES: Shirodhara, craniosacral therapy, moxibustion

RELAXATION PRACTICES: Walking meditation, martial arts, fiery crafts

ESSENTIAL OILS: Ginger, vetiver, black pepper

FLOWER ESSENCES: Impatiens, tiger lily, larkspur

YOGA POSES: Wide-legged Forward Bend (*Prasarita Padottanasana*), Warrior I (*Virabhadrasana* I), Head-to-Knee Forward Bend (*Janu Sirsasana*)

STELLAR REFLECTIONS

What I'm really passionate about right now is:

....

....

....

....

....

These are the things worth fighting for:

....

....

....

....

....

What really energizes me is:

....

....

....

....

....

Taurus

CHARACTERISTICS: Creative, grounded, kindhearted, patient, practical, predictable, security oriented, self-indulgent, sensual, serene, steadfast, stubborn

PERSONAL HEALTH PROFILE: A Taurus has a hardy constitution and great physical resources. When it comes to keeping you well, your resilience is a strong asset. Remember that sudden change is often a stressor for Taurus; giving yourself time to slowly shift your rhythm and adapt to new things can keep you relaxed and inspire your well-being.

WELLNESS THERAPIES: Aromatherapy massage, sound therapy, food-based body treatments

RELAXATION PRACTICES: Pottery, communing with nature, music

ESSENTIAL OILS: Vanilla, palmarosa, thyme

FLOWER ESSENCES: Chestnut bud, iris, hound's tongue

YOGA POSES: Cow (*Bitilasana*), Bridge (*Setu Bandha Sarvangasana*), Staff (*Dandasana*)

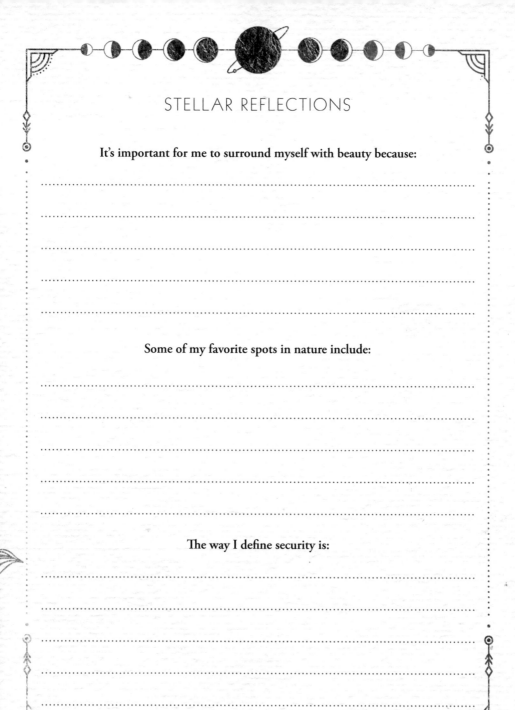

STELLAR REFLECTIONS

It's important for me to surround myself with beauty because:

....

....

....

....

....

Some of my favorite spots in nature include:

....

....

....

....

....

The way I define security is:

....

....

....

....

Gemini

CHARACTERISTICS: Adaptable, cunning, curious, dual-natured, fickle, informative, mercurial, observant, quick-witted, spontaneous, talkative, youthful

PERSONAL HEALTH PROFILE: A Gemini loves to solve problems of all kinds, and those involving your health are no exception. With your keen curiosity and need-to-know nature, you'll wade through books, websites, and medical journals—and pick the brain of anyone in the know—in your quest to find the best treatment plan to cure your ailment or enhance your well-being.

WELLNESS THERAPIES: Manicures, chair massage, talk therapy

RELAXATION PRACTICES: Games and puzzles, pranayama, journaling

ESSENTIAL OILS: Rosemary, lavender, eucalyptus

FLOWER ESSENCES: White chestnut, cosmos, cerato

YOGA POSES: Cobra (*Bhujangasana*), Extended Side Angle (*Utthita Parsvakonasana*), Dolphin (*Ardha Pincha Mayurasana*)

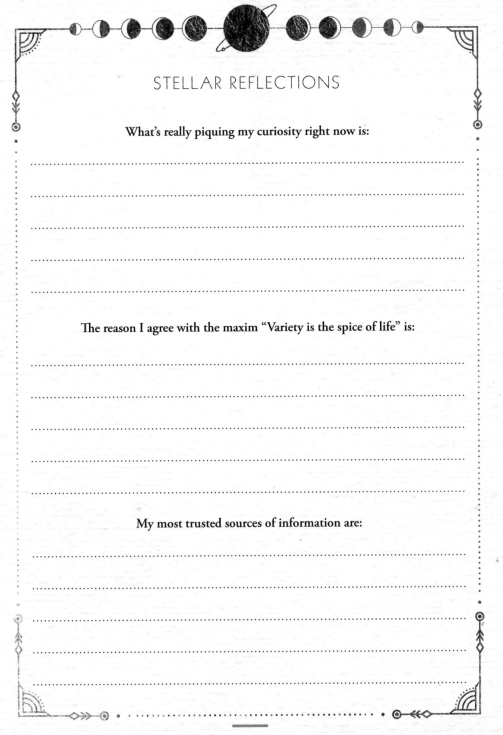

STELLAR REFLECTIONS

What's really piquing my curiosity right now is:

....

....

....

....

....

The reason I agree with the maxim "Variety is the spice of life" is:

....

....

....

....

....

My most trusted sources of information are:

....

....

....

....

Cancer

CHARACTERISTICS: Defensive, emotional, gentle, hospitable, indirect, kind, moody, nostalgic, nurturing, protective, sensitive, traditional

PERSONAL HEALTH PROFILE: While the Crab, your astrological totem, has a defensive shell, within you resides a very sensitive soul whose physical health is highly influenced by an expansive reservoir of feelings. Accepting and expressing your emotions, rather than fearing and internalizing them, can do wonders for your health.

WELLNESS THERAPIES: Java lulur, hydrotherapy, milk bath

RELAXATION PRACTICES: Regular "me time," genealogy projects, aquatic fitness classes

ESSENTIAL OILS: Jasmine, hyssop, clary sage

FLOWER ESSENCES: Baby blue eyes, clematis, honeysuckle

YOGA POSES: Standing Forward Bend (*Uttanasana*), Easy Pose with Alternate Nostril Breathing (*Sukhasana/Nadi Shodhana*), Legs-Up-the-Wall (*Viparita Karani*)

STELLAR REFLECTIONS

My favorite ways to nurture myself include:

....

....

....

....

....

The people and/or things I feel most called to protect are:

....

....

....

....

....

Here's how I've come to trust my emotions:

....

....

....

....

....

Leo

CHARACTERISTICS: Charismatic, cheerful, courageous, dignified, dramatic, expressive, faithful, forthright, magnanimous, proud, warmhearted, winsome

PERSONAL HEALTH PROFILE: Leos radiate an incandescent sense of wellness and vivacity. Roaring with stamina, you energetically participate in the many experiences life presents to you, including those that allow you to share your creative and shining self with the world.

WELLNESS THERAPIES: Hot stone massage, biofeedback, hair and scalp treatments

RELAXATION PRACTICES: Sunbathing, child's play, acting

ESSENTIAL OILS: German chamomile, neroli, lemon

FLOWER ESSENCES: Borage, Indian paintbrush, sunflower

YOGA POSES: Lion (*Simhasana*),
Cat (*Marjaryasana*),
Sphinx (*Salamba Bhujangasana*)

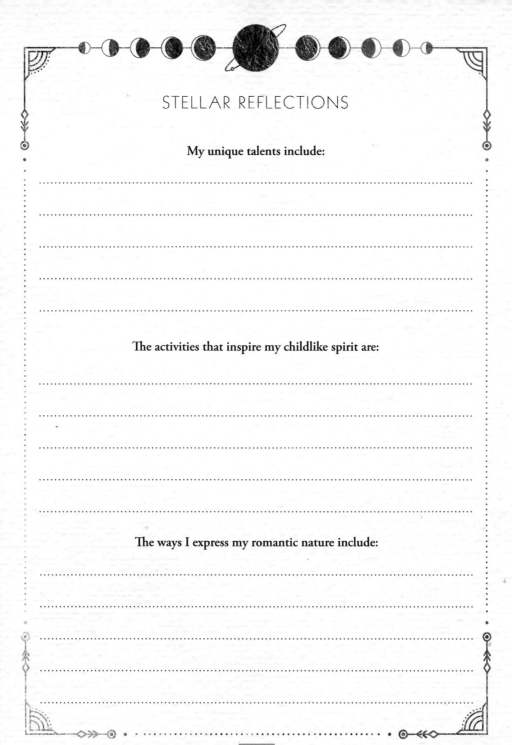

STELLAR REFLECTIONS

My unique talents include:

....
....
....
....
....

The activities that inspire my childlike spirit are:

....
....
....
....
....

The ways I express my romantic nature include:

....
....
....
....
....

Virgo

CHARACTERISTICS: Analytical, anxious, critical, detailed, diligent, efficient, helpful, logical, orderly, precise, rational, tidy

PERSONAL HEALTH PROFILE: Virgo is associated with health consciousness, with people born under this sign diligently focused on being well and staying well. Yet, since Virgos are perfectionists, your idea of wellness may be a bit more exacting than others. Detail-oriented Virgos are hyperaware of all their body's signs and signals; if anything seems even slightly amiss, you notice it and want to remedy it.

WELLNESS THERAPIES: Fasting, steam baths, herbal wraps

RELAXATION PRACTICES: Crafting, gardening, animal companionship

ESSENTIAL OILS: Melissa, cardamom, carrot seed

FLOWER ESSENCES: Pine, centaury, rock water

YOGA POSES: Seated Forward Bend (*Paschimottanasana*), Half Lord of the Fishes (*Ardha Matsyendrasana*), Extended Puppy (*Uttana Shishosana*)

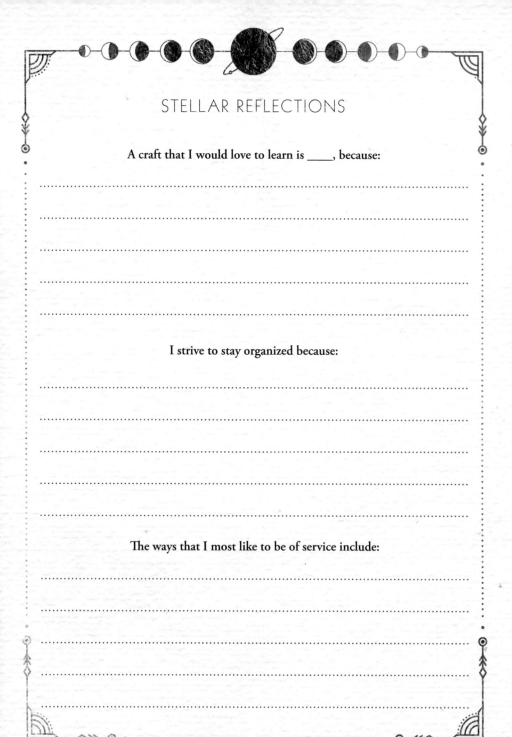

STELLAR REFLECTIONS

A craft that I would love to learn is _____, because:

....

....

....

....

....

I strive to stay organized because:

....

....

....

....

....

The ways that I most like to be of service include:

....

....

....

....

....

Libra

CHARACTERISTICS: Charming, diplomatic, equitable, gracious, indecisive, judicious, orderly, poised, romantic, sociable, stylish, sybaritic

PERSONAL HEALTH PROFILE: Libras dislike when things are out of balance, including their health. Since you appreciate the beauty of harmony, any physical sign or symptom that leaves you feeling less than peaceful—even one that would be perceived as inconsequential to most—registers strongly on the Libran wellness scale.

WELLNESS THERAPIES: Facials, sugar body polish, lomilomi massage

RELAXATION PRACTICES: Feng shui, tai chi, writing poetry

ESSENTIAL OILS: Damask rose, rose geranium, peppermint

FLOWER ESSENCES: Scleranthus, scarlet monkeyflower, pretty face

YOGA POSES: Tree (*Vrksasana*), Lord of the Dance (*Natarajasana*), Boat (*Navasana*)

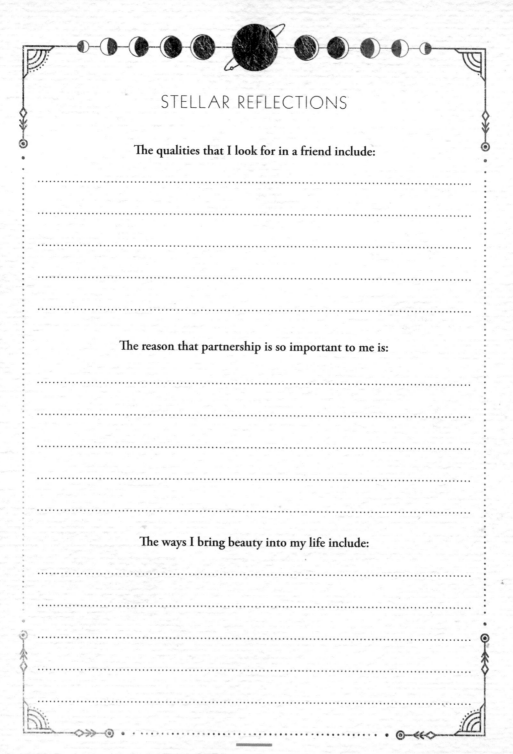

STELLAR REFLECTIONS

The qualities that I look for in a friend include:

....

....

....

....

....

The reason that partnership is so important to me is:

....

....

....

....

....

The ways I bring beauty into my life include:

....

....

....

....

Scorpio

CHARACTERISTICS: Brooding, complex, determined, emotional, forceful, intense, passionate, probing, regenerative, resilient, resourceful, secretive

PERSONAL HEALTH PROFILE: Scorpios have incredible regenerative abilities that can serve as powerful allies in their personal health care. You have a cogent capacity to heal yourself, aided by a deep-seated awareness that your mind and emotions play an inextricable role in your physical well-being.

WELLNESS THERAPIES: Structural integration, colonics, flotation tanks

RELAXATION PRACTICES: Neo-tantra, solving mysteries, mud treatment

ESSENTIAL OILS: Ylang-ylang, basil, helichrysum

FLOWER ESSENCES: Holly, mustard, basil

YOGA POSES: Garland (*Malasana*), Wide-angle Seated Forward Bend (*Upavistha Konasana*), Dead Bug (*Ananda Balasana*)

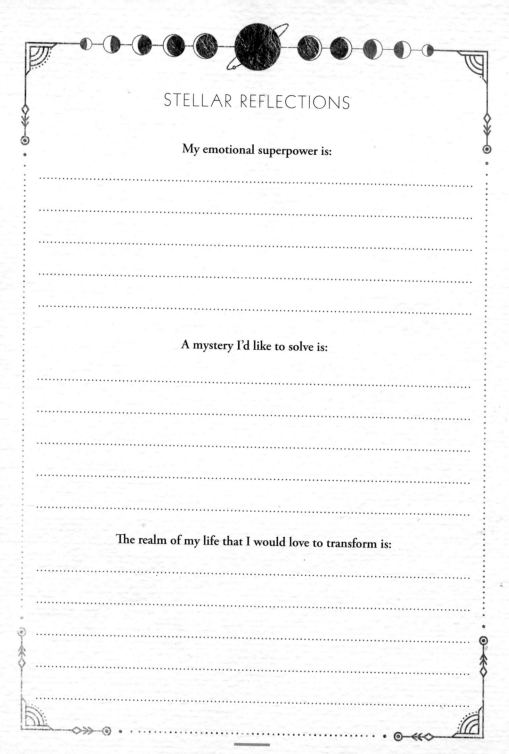

STELLAR REFLECTIONS

My emotional superpower is:

....

....

....

....

....

A mystery I'd like to solve is:

....

....

....

....

....

The realm of my life that I would love to transform is:

....

....

....

....

....

Sagittarius

CHARACTERISTICS: Adventurous, dogmatic, exuberant, inspired, jovial, optimistic, philosophical, upbeat, versatile, visionary, wise, zealous

PERSONAL HEALTH PROFILE: As with everything in your life, you are apt to take a philosophical approach to your health. With "why" as one of your favorite words, you may question, for example, why you may experience certain health challenges or why one wellness approach works more effectively for you than another. Your inquiring nature helps you pursue answers that will elevate your well-being.

WELLNESS THERAPIES: Thai massage, Pilates, equine-assisted psychotherapy

RELAXATION PRACTICES: Creative visualization, sports-training programs, travel

ESSENTIAL OILS: Juniper, grapefruit, nutmeg

FLOWER ESSENCES: Vervain, rabbitbrush, angelica

YOGA POSES: Warrior II (*Virabhadrasana II*), Fire Log (*Agnistambhasana*), High Lunge (*Utthita Ashwa Sanchalanasana*)

STELLAR REFLECTIONS

A subject I'm really interested in learning more about is:

....
....
....
....
....

Something that I'm very enthusiastic about right now is:

....
....
....
....
....

My core beliefs include:

....
....
....
....

Capricorn

CHARACTERISTICS: Ambitious, committed, conservative, disciplined, frugal, hardworking, loyal, persistent, pragmatic, sarcastic, straightforward, structured

PERSONAL HEALTH PROFILE: With ardent strength in the face of adversity, you are not likely to complain about your health or any aches and pains you may feel. This may help you power through the limitations that would stop others. Yet a great source of your personal healing can come from knowing that sometimes other people's knowledge can benefit you and asking for help isn't a sign of weakness.

WELLNESS THERAPIES: Swedish massage, body-moisturizing treatments, Feldenkrais method

RELAXATION PRACTICES: Hiking, labyrinth walking, frolic and play

ESSENTIAL OILS: Scotch pine, cypress, frankincense

FLOWER ESSENCES: Oak, mimulus, vine

YOGA POSES: Mountain (*Tadasana*), Chair (*Utkatasana*), Hero (*Virasana*)

STELLAR REFLECTIONS

My three-year plan is:

....

....

....

....

....

The people to whom I am most loyal are:

....

....

....

....

....

I hope my legacy will be:

....

....

....

....

....

Aquarius

CHARACTERISTICS: Altruistic, cerebral, detached, eccentric, egalitarian, friendly, independent, innovative, perceptive, philanthropic, progressive, rebellious

PERSONAL HEALTH PROFILE: Aquarius is a sign that embodies great vitality. You maintain a dynamic energy and sense of composure that can translate into sustained good health. With your highly perceptive mind, you frequently have out-of-the-blue flashes of insight, many of which you can use to amplify your well-being.

WELLNESS THERAPIES: NIA technique, acupuncture, reiki

RELAXATION PRACTICES: Qigong, mineral salt bath, volunteering

ESSENTIAL OILS: Patchouli, sweet marjoram, benzoin

FLOWER ESSENCES: California wild rose, dill, quaking grass

YOGA POSES: Downward-facing Dog (*Adho Mukha Savasana*), Noose (*Pashasana*), Reclining Big Toe (*Supta Padangusthasana*)

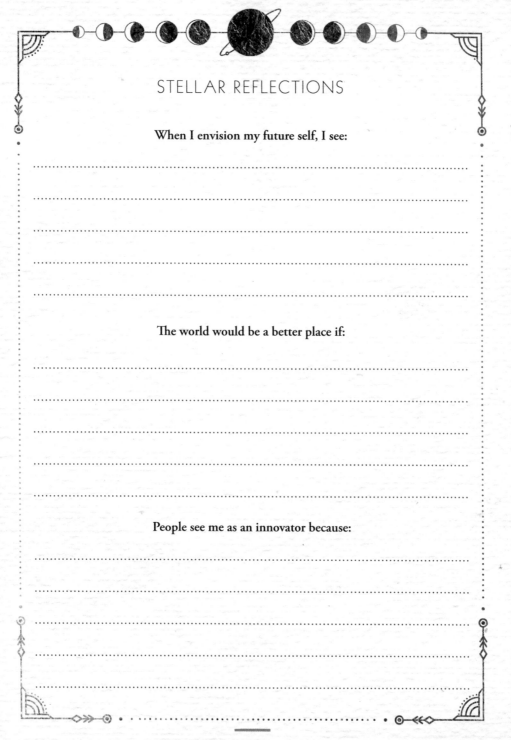

STELLAR REFLECTIONS

When I envision my future self, I see:

....

....

....

....

....

The world would be a better place if:

....

....

....

....

....

People see me as an innovator because:

....

....

....

....

....

Pisces

CHARACTERISTICS: Dreamy, elusive, empathetic, forgiving, idealistic, imaginative, impressionable, poetic, psychic, selfless, spacey, spiritual

PERSONAL HEALTH PROFILE: You have a tendency to experience the world in a more holistic and poetic way than others; that's one of the reasons that Pisces seems especially open to mind-body-spirit approaches to healing. With an empathetic nature, you like to be of service; just make sure you don't give away too much time, energy, or emotion to others or it can impact your vitality.

WELLNESS THERAPIES: Watsu, reflexology, hypnotherapy

RELAXATION PRACTICES: Meditation, swimming, walking

ESSENTIAL OILS: Sandalwood, myrrh, tea tree

FLOWER ESSENCES: Nicotiana, aspen, pink yarrow

YOGA POSES: Fish (*Matsyasana*), Child (*Balasana*), Toe Crunch

STELLAR REFLECTIONS

Here's how I define love:

....

....

....

....

....

I know I need to establish better boundaries when:

....

....

....

....

....

The last random act of kindness I performed was:

....

....

....

....

....

Celestial Event Calendar

THE MOONS

January 2, 2022: Capricorn New Moon
January 17, 2022: Cancer Full Moon
February 1, 2022: Aquarius New Moon
February 16, 2022: Leo Full Moon
March 2, 2022: Pisces New Moon
March 18, 2022: Virgo Full Moon
April 1, 2022: Aries New Moon
April 16, 2022: Libra Full Moon
April 30, 2022: Taurus New Moon (Solar Eclipse)
May 16, 2022: Scorpio Full Moon (Lunar Eclipse)
May 30, 2022: Gemini New Moon
June 14, 2022: Sagittarius Full Moon
June 28, 2022: Cancer New Moon
July 13, 2022: Capricorn Full Moon
July 28, 2022: Leo New Moon
August 11, 2022: Aquarius Full Moon
August 27, 2022: Virgo New Moon
September 10, 2022: Pisces Full Moon
September 25, 2022: Libra New Moon
October 9, 2022: Aries Full Moon
October 25, 2022: Scorpio New Moon (Solar Eclipse)
November 8, 2022: Taurus Full Moon (Lunar Eclipse)
November 23, 2022: Sagittarius New Moon
December 7, 2022: Gemini Full Moon
December 23, 2022: Capricorn New Moon

January 6, 2023: Cancer Full Moon
January 21, 2023: Aquarius New Moon
February 5, 2023: Leo Full Moon
February 20, 2023: Pisces New Moon
March 7, 2023: Virgo Full Moon
March 21, 2023: Aries New Moon
April 6, 2023: Libra Full Moon
April 20, 2023: Aries New Moon (Solar Eclipse)
May 5, 2023: Scorpio Full Moon (Lunar Eclipse)
May 19, 2023: Taurus New Moon
June 3, 2023: Sagittarius Full Moon
June 18, 2023: Gemini New Moon
July 3, 2023: Capricorn Full Moon

July 17, 2023: Cancer New Moon
August 1, 2023: Aquarius Full Moon
August 16, 2023: Leo New Moon
August 30, 2023: Pisces Full Moon
September 14, 2023: Virgo New Moon
September 29, 2023: Aries Full Moon
October 14, 2023: Libra New Moon (Solar Eclipse)
October 28, 2023: Taurus Full Moon (Lunar Eclipse)
November 13, 2023: Scorpio New Moon
November 27, 2023: Gemini Full Moon
December 12, 2023: Sagittarius New Moon
December 26, 2023: Cancer Full Moon

January 11, 2024: Capricorn New Moon
January 25, 2024: Leo Full Moon
February 9, 2024: Aquarius New Moon
February 24, 2024: Virgo Full Moon
March 10, 2024: Pisces New Moon
March 25, 2024: Libra Full Moon (Lunar Eclipse)
April 8, 2024: Aries New Moon (Solar Eclipse)
April 23, 2024: Scorpio Full Moon
May 7, 2024: Taurus New Moon
May 23, 2024: Sagittarius Full Moon
June 6, 2024: Gemini New Moon
June 21, 2024: Capricorn Full Moon
July 5, 2024: Cancer New Moon
July 21, 2024: Capricorn Full Moon
August 4, 2024: Leo New Moon
August 19, 2024: Aquarius Full Moon
September 2, 2024: Virgo New Moon
September 17, 2024: Pisces Full Moon (Lunar Eclipse)
October 2, 2024: Libra New Moon (Solar Eclipse)
October 17, 2024: Aries Full Moon
November 1, 2024: Scorpio New Moon
November 15, 2024: Taurus Full Moon
December 1, 2024: Sagittarius New Moon
December 15, 2024: Gemini Full Moon
December 30, 2024: Capricorn New Moon

MERCURY RETROGRADE

January 14, 2022 – February 3, 2022
May 10, 2022 – June 3, 2022
September 9, 2022 – October 2, 2022
December 29, 2022 – January 18, 2023
April 21, 2023 – May 14, 2023
August 23, 2023 – September 15, 2023
December 13, 2023 – January 1, 2024
April 1, 2024 – April 25, 2024
August 5, 2024 – August 28, 2024
November 25, 2024 – December 15, 2024

VENUS RETROGRADE

December 19, 2021 – January 29, 2022
July 22, 2023 – September 3, 2023

MARS RETROGRADE

October 30, 2022 – January 12, 2023
December 6, 2024 – February 23, 2025

JUPITER STATION

July 28, 2022: Stations retrograde
November 23, 2022: Stations direct
September 4, 2023: Stations retrograde
December 30, 2023: Stations direct
October 9, 2024: Stations retrograde

SATURN STATION

June 4, 2022: Stations retrograde
October 23, 2022: Stations direct
June 17, 2023: Stations retrograde
November 4, 2023: Stations direct
June 29, 2024: Stations retrograde
November 15, 2024: Stations direct

URANUS STATION

January 18, 2022: Stations direct
August 24, 2022: Stations retrograde
January 22, 2023: Stations direct
August 28, 2023: Stations retrograde
January 27, 2024: Stations direct
September 1, 2024: Stations retrograde

NEPTUNE STATION

June 28, 2022: Stations retrograde
December 3, 2022: Stations direct
June 30, 2023: Stations retrograde
December 6, 2023: Stations direct
July 2, 2024: Stations retrograde
December 7, 2024: Stations direct

PLUTO STATION

April 29, 2022: Stations retrograde
October 8, 2022: Stations direct
May 1, 2023: Stations retrograde
October 10, 2023: Stations direct
May 2, 2024: Stations retrograde
October 11, 2024: Stations direct

Inspiring | Educating | Creating | Entertaining

Brimming with creative inspiration, how-to projects, and useful information to enrich your everyday life, Quarto Knows is a favorite destination for those pursuing their interests and passions. Visit our site and dig deeper with our books into your area of interest: Quarto Creates, Quarto Cooks, Quarto Homes, Quarto Lives, Quarto Drives, Quarto Explores, Quarto Gifts, or Quarto Kids.

Rock Point titles are also available at discount for retail, wholesale, promotional, and bulk purchase. For details, contact the Special Sales Manager by email at specialsales@quarto.com or by mail at The Quarto Group, Attn: Special Sales Manager, 100 Cummings Center, Suite 265D, Beverly, MA 01915 USA.

10 9 8 7 6 5 4 3 2 1

ISBN: 978-1-63106-833-1

Publisher: Rage Kindelsperger
Creative Director: Laura Drew
Managing Editor: Cara Donaldson
Senior Editor: Katharine Moore
Cover Design: Andrea Ho
Layout Design: Laura Shaw Design, Inc.

Printed in China

This journal provides general information on various widely known and widely accepted topics that tend to evoke feelings of strength and confidence. However, it should not be relied upon as recommending or promoting any specific diagnosis or method of treatment for a particular condition, and it is not intended as a substitute for medical advice or for direct diagnosis and treatment of a medical condition by a qualified physician. Readers who have questions about a particular condition, possible treatments for that condition, or possible reactions from the condition or its treatment should consult a physician or other qualified health-care professional.